Gifts of a Stranger

Gifts of a Stranger

A Convert's Round-the-World Travels
and Spiritual Journeys

Ahuvah Gray

TARGUM/FELDHEIM

First published 2004
Copyright © 2004 by Ahuvah Gray
ISBN 1-56871-331-2

Published by:
TARGUM PRESS, INC.
22700 W. Eleven Mile Rd.
Southfield, MI 48034
E-mail: targum@netvision.net.il
Fax: 888-298-9992
www.targum.com

Distributed by:
FELDHEIM PUBLISHERS
208 Airport Executive Park
Nanuet, NY 10954

Printing plates: "Frank," Jerusalem

Printed in Israel

To contact the author, please write to Ahuvabasyisroel@hotmail.com
or see www.mysisterthejew.com.

Rabbi Aryeh Carmel

Dear Reader,

Ten years ago Ahuvah Gray entered the community of Bayit Vegan as a stranger. Today she is highly respected and loved by all who know her as she travels worldwide inspiring Jews to daven and say *Tehillim* "from the heart."

Once a stranger, Ahuvah is now a daughter of Israel as well as an accomplished authoress.

Her first book, *My Sister, the Jew*, describes her experiences in becoming a righteous proselyte, following in the footsteps of Ruth the Moabitess. This, her second book, is entitled *Gifts of a Stranger*.

It is my hope that this book will inspire Jews everywhere to daven and say *Tehillim* as sincerely and fervently as she does. If so, this will certainly prove to be a most precious gift.

Rabbi Aryeh Carmel

Rebbetzin Tziporah Heller

Once more it has been my pleasure to enter Ahuvah Gray's world. It is a world in which even the ordinary events that fill the day take on the shadow of Hashem's providence and love. The reason for this is that the author conveys to us a sense of the world as she sees it. She writes and speaks with simplicity and without any sort of pretension, but her message can't help but touch anyone who can open their heart to her story. One of the most significant episodes of the book concerns a South African girl, Shira, who changes her entire view of who she is and what life is about from her exposure to Ms. Gray. It wasn't the brilliance of her rhetoric that made the difference, but the truth that she spoke with such rare personal credibility.

Anyone who reads this book is going to find themselves subtly changed and enjoy every moment of the journey.

Tziporah Heller

Rebbetzin Tziporah Heller

In loving memory of my grandparents

Sylvester and Ola C. Gray

who laid the foundation for my spiritual well-being
and continue to nourish my soul to this day.

Willie and Lelar Franklin

who taught me morals and ethics that were a plumb line
throughout my business career.

"Train the youth according to his way.
Even when he grows old, he will not swerve from it"
(*Mishlei* 22:6).

Contents

Spiritual Journeys & 135

Foreword

By Sheina Medwed

Six years ago, Ahuvah Gray illuminated the threshold of my
home with her grace, her beauty, her mischievously
dimpled smile, and her deep love of God. As I listened to the
story of her spiritual journey, I said, "You have to write a book."
The outgrowth of that statement can be found in her last book,
My Sister, the Jew.

Although it is a mitzvah not to covet, I must admit to feeling
a twinge of jealousy for the readers who have had the privilege
of buying this book and savoring Ahuvah's thoughts, stories,
and inspiring impressions for the first time. I envy them their
first experience with Ahuvah, traveling with her around the
world and finally arriving with her at the center of that world,
Jerusalem — may we see it rebuilt speedily, in our lifetimes.

But if I cannot share the enjoyment of a reader first experi-
encing this book, I can still rejoice that Hashem, in His kind-

ness, has granted me the privilege of watching the process of writing this second book with Ahuvah. I have deepened my love and admiration for the pure wellspring of her being, which is nurtured and developed by a deep love for Hashem, His Torah, His people, His city, and His land. Ahuvah lives in the Torah and her daily prayers. As such, she is able to have Torah and *tefillah* live through her very being and inspire and touch the lives of thousands in the international network of the Jewish world today.

Although the title of this book is *Gifts of a Stranger*, for me this process has been the gift of a beloved friend.

May Hashem bless Ahuvah, among all the Jewish people, with health and strength to continue her work. May He answer all the prayers of her heart for good, for life, and for peace, and may we all rejoice together with *klal Yisrael* in the coming of Mashiach and the rebuilding of the Beis HaMikdash, speedily in our days. Amen.

Sheina Medwed is the author of *A Mother's Favorite Stories* (ArtScroll/Mesorah Publications, 1998) and the forthcoming book *Live, Remember, Tell the World: The Story of Leah Kaufman, Hidden Child Survivor of Transnitria*.

Introduction

The Metamorphosis of Ahuvah Gray

by Sarah Shapiro

As I follow Ahuvah Gray along the narrow stairway leading to her apartment, and step up into the little light-filled penthouse that is her home above the rooftops of Bayit Vegan, what comes to mind is the childhood classic *A Little Princess* by Frances Hodgson Burnett. In that famous tale, the heroine dwells cozily in an attic room above the rooftops of London, and looks out from her oasis upon the world below. Here, through windows on every side, it's the fast-moving clouds of a rainy winter morning in Israel that adorn the horizon, and the branches of a Jerusalem pine tree that brush up against the opaquely luminous rectangle of skylight.

Ahuvah Gray herself — a black American who was once a Christian minister and is now an Orthodox Jew — does look, in fact, like some exotic sort of princess, with her high-cheekboned delicacy, and long hair, and regal bearing.

"Just look at this," she exclaims, opening the door to her porch and gesturing me outside into the damp, brisk air. "Isn't this something?" Far off on the distant skyline to our right lie the walls of the Old City under the receding storm, and way over to the east, the dimly visible mountains of Jordan looming like gray mist over the Dead Sea. "This view from my porch always reminds me of sitting on my grandmother's lap when I was four years old, in Mound Bayou, Mississippi — that's when she first started teaching us children the psalms of King David. She'd recite Psalm 24:1, 'The earth is the Lord's and the fullness thereof, the world, and they that dwell therein.' Here I am, and I still can't believe my eyes after all these years — the goodness of the Lord in the land of the living, and I always think, *Thank you, Grandmother, for such a beautiful gift.*"

Back inside, serving me tea, Ahuvah Gray speaks of that woman, the one who started her on the long journey that ultimately brought her to Israel, and to the Jewish people, and to Judaism.

"My paternal grandmother was my role model. All I remember of her was the *chesed* she did all day long. She was always cooking food for sick people and bringing it to them. And my mother, God bless her soul, she was my other role model. Throughout my childhood she would bring homeless people to our table. One time there was an old guy she brought in — our table was hardly ever just us, it was always poor people sitting down with us — and my sister Nellie made a face from the smell of that man. My mother gave her a look, and told her to never again do or say anything that could insult one of our guests. Today Nellie — she lives in L. A. — she's been doing the same thing now for the last twenty years, taking care of the poor and the homeless.

"I was born and raised in Chicago, but when we were growing up, my parents would take us every summer to visit Grandmother in Mound Bayou, which was a small all-black town. Now, years later when I was working for Continental Airlines — at first I was a stewardess, then a flight attendant supervisor, then I moved into sales and marketing, where I was able to make up my own work schedule — every summer I'd make that trip to Mound Bayou to see Grandmother the way we always had when we were small. One summer morning when I arrived at her house and went looking for her, I saw that the door to her bedroom was standing open and that my grandmother, who was seventy-eight at the time, was kneeling down by her bed praying fervently — she always turned up the volume, so to speak. I stood there by the door completely mesmerized for I don't know how long, and I finally said, 'Grandmother, at your age are you still getting down on your knees to pray?' She looked up and said, 'Delores, this is the way I've prayed my whole life. It's the only way I know.'

"That was one of the most important moments in my life. It was a turning point. I was already a minister then, but that experience at the door to my grandmother's room gave me the stamina to commit my life to prayer."

I ask her what that means in practical terms.

"It means that I committed myself to have a designated time and place for prayer. The time was at five in the morning, and the place was under the blankets of my bed. That was the great thing about that job, I didn't have to be at any office at nine o'clock — so I'd just pull the blanket up over my head and pray for hours; it was my favorite part of the day, every day. It still is. It takes me forever to go through the entire morning service in Hebrew and I love every minute of it. In any case, as I was saying, from that experience, seeing my elderly grandmother on her knees in prayer, from that moment on, I have had a life of prayer."

"Under the blankets, you were in your own little synagogue?"

"Right. My own little synagogue. In those days, though, I didn't know anything about the Jewish way of davening *shacharis, minchah, maariv*. But I had read in the Book of Psalms that King David prayed three times a day and I said to myself, 'If that's how King David prayed, then I'm going to pray three times a day, too.'

"After my grandmother died a few years later, I started having a difficult time with Christian dogma. Now, when you're the minister of a Christian congregation, that's not the sort of thing you go around saying, so I kept it to myself as long as I could, until finally I had to publicly declare that I could no longer remain in the ministry. It simply did not seem like truth to me anymore.

"When I resigned from the ministry, I had no thought whatsoever of becoming a Jew. It wasn't on my mind at all. But ever since I was a teenager, I had felt an affinity for Jewish people. I had felt that affinity starting back when I was in seventh grade and had my first job working in the dress shop of a family named Greenberg. They used to invite me to their house for the Shabbos meals. I continued working for them until the Chicago riots, when their store was looted and trashed and they had to give up their business.

"I loved the Greenbergs and they loved me. We were like one family. I used to go there for Shabbos and then I'd go home and tell my mother all about it — what they were like, and that they had this funny-looking bread. The only thing I didn't tell her was that they had wine. She would have *plotzed*, because my mother, may she rest in peace, she never had a drink in her life.

"That was my introduction to Jewish people, and from that time on, whenever Jewish holidays came around, I had this desire to be with Jewish people. And whenever I was in a bookstore, if there was a book in there about Jews or Judaism, it always caught my eye and I'd buy it.

"Long before the idea of conversion ever occurred to me, in my own prayers I'd stopped addressing God as three gods in one, the Trinity — it made no sense to me. It didn't seem real. But I had found a church that kept the Sabbath on the seventh day instead of on Sunday — it was called the Straitway Church. One day this Jewish woman visited it and we started talking. That was Ruth Sharon, who wanted to find ways to bring about understanding between blacks and Jews. One day the minister said to us that he was going to have us imagine being at Mount Sinai when God gave the Ten Commandments, so he led us through this visualization.

"I can't convey what I experienced that day. I'll just tell you that when he was done, I opened my eyes and there was Ruth, looking at me, and I said, 'Ruth, I was there,' and she said, 'I know, Delores.'

"The two of us, Ruth and I, we ended up working together. We organized an annual Passover tour to Israel for Christians and Jews together."

I tell Ahuvah that I remember reading about that in the *Jerusalem Post* years ago.

"Yes, they wrote about it. It was eye-catching, you know,

that Christians and Jews were doing this together. But it was during those early years in Israel that I experienced another turning point. On one particular trip, I had taken a group up north to the ancient city of Tzefas, and we were touring the old synagogues when I saw a Jewish siddur, a prayer book. Now I didn't really know what a Jewish prayer book was but I had always wanted to see one, so I picked it up to take a look. I started reading. I read *Shema Yisrael*, God is One. And it struck me: These are powerful. These are powerful prayers."

"So was it while you were on those Passover tours that you decided to convert?"

"No, I can't say it started then. With hindsight, I see how everything in my childhood, everything I experienced in my adult life, it was all pointing toward this, every part of it. When Ruth and I first joined together for the tours, she said to me, 'Now, there's just one thing, Delores, that I've got to tell you. You must never try to convert me,' and I said, 'Don't you worry about it!' She had no idea yet that that was just about the farthest thing from my mind!"

I give a laugh. "Little did she know, *she* was going to convert *you*!"

"No, that didn't happen either. Nobody converted me. Truth just became obvious, that's all I can say. And once I realized in what direction I had to go, I could no longer conduct the tours as a Christian. I was sorry to leave Ruth — she was happy for me but felt she had lost a good liaison between Christians and Jews, because as a Christian minister, I was able to say things other people weren't. Christians trusted me. They listened when I told them that it was not the Jews who killed their messiah, and some of the other things they believe that are in part responsible for anti-Semitism. But *baruch Hashem*, I found my way, with God's help."

"What was your reaction upon learning, later on, that according to Jewish tradition, the gesture of bowing down is reserved only for the Yom Kippur service?"

"It was very humbling. When I learned how to daven according to Jewish tradition, what was amazing to me was that although we prostrate ourselves on Yom Kippur in order to get closer to God, because it's such a powerful gesture, other than that we do not. Other than that, a Jew does not have to place himself in that position."

"It's common knowledge that ever since the sixties and early seventies, when so many Jews were involved with the Civil Rights Movement, there has been a strange love/hate relationship between the two groups. From your present standpoint, Ahuvah, so what do you think it is, between blacks and Jews?"

"Look, in my family, I was brought up to believe that no man is better or worse than another, that we are all, every single one of us, children of God. I love my skin. I love the color of my skin. But I was brought up to believe that I am neither inferior nor superior."

"So it must be that that religious viewpoint is so deeply ingrained in you, Ahuvah, that you're not conflicted about inferiority/superiority. So you bring that out in others. 'As water reflects the face, so does one heart reflect another.' "

"Well, I don't know. A few times, people have said to me, 'Oh, it must be so hard for you in that *chareidi* community, being a black convert. Don't you encounter a lot of racial prejudice?' I just have to tell them, 'My dears, I have never in my life been given as much love.'

"That love from the Orthodox community started right when I decided to convert. I had run into a catch-22. In order to convert, it was required that I study at an Orthodox institution. Yet in order to enter an Orthodox institution I had to be Jewish! Nonetheless, there was a women's learning center called Nishmat that accepted me as a student. That place is run by one of the most amazing women one could ever hope to meet, Rebbetzin Henkin. She had the amazing ability to nurture and mother every girl in that seminary.

"After learning for a year in Nishmat, the momentous day of my conversion arrived. It was an important day, to say the least, and I decided that after going to the *mikveh*, I was going to celebrate by going downtown and treating myself to a nice meal. However, one of the *rebbetzins* was very emphatic that I should come back to the *beis midrash* of the seminary afterwards. So after the *mikveh*, I went back to the seminary's *beis midrash* and when I entered, there was a huge sign that said, '*Siman tov vemazal tov.*'

"I'll remember that day as long as I live. The American girls and the Israeli girls were all singing '*Siman tov, mazal tov,*' and their voices, mingled together, sounded like an opera, or a symphony. They asked me to make a speech and the only thing I could think to say was, 'I don't think I've ever experienced such love before in my life. I think I'm beginning to understand the love between God and the Jewish people.'

"I've met converts from all over the world, and our stories are all the same although our faces and backgrounds are different. My roommate from Neve Yerushalayim was from Singapore. I've met converts from Germany, and Africa, from the Philippines, but we all have one heartbeat. We couldn't rest un-

til we found our way to Judaism and Jewish observance. When I
lecture I tell my audience that you can take a Jewish *neshamah*
and put it into any *kli* (vessel). But that *neshamah* will not rest
until it finds its way to *Yiddishkeit*."

The interview seems to have come to a close. As I'm getting
ready to go, I tell Ahuvah Gray what her apartment reminded me of when I first walked in.

"Oh, this apartment. That's a story. For another time. All I
can say is, Hashem gave me exactly what I needed. He always
has and always will."

"How do you account for your *emunah*?" I ask her.

"You have *emunah*, too, you know. Sometimes we just don't
realize what we have. As I told you, I witnessed my grandmother's faith throughout my life and it was passed on, definitely. And almost as far back as I can remember, I've always
put things into what I think of as my God Box."

I asked what that is.

"Well, I'll give you an example. One night around five years
ago, not long after I got this apartment, the telephone rang at 4
a.m. Now, anybody who lives far away from his family can tell
you that anything like that's going to make you nervous. When I
left America I left my entire family behind — I haven't seen them
for four years now — and so as I reached for the phone I was already dreading whatever I was going to hear. It was my sister
Nellie, and sure enough, she had bad news. Our beloved brother,
Ezra — a young man, he's my baby brother — had had a massive
heart attack.

"When I hung up that phone, I started davening. I davened,
and davened, and kept davening, and crying. I was begging God till

the sun came up. 'Please, Hashem, save Ezra. Don't let Ezra die.'

"Then all of a sudden, it hit me. I thought to myself, *Wait a minute*, and I said, 'For heaven's sake, what in the world am I doing? Who am I to tell God what to do?'

"So then, I prayed, 'Hashem, You formed Ezra in our mother's womb. You created him, You formed him. It's You who gave him his soul. It's You who gave him life. So if it's time for You to take him back, I let go. I let go, Hashem.' That's how I put Ezra in my God Box. And then I added, 'And let Nellie get it.' "

"Let Nellie get it?"

"Right, I said, 'Hashem, let Nellie get it.' "

"Did she get it?"

"She got it."

"And Ezra...?"

"Oh, he's fine. Nellie called me after three days to say he was sitting up in bed cracking jokes. Look, all of this is my way of expressing the concept of the Yitzchak principle, when Avraham was going to sacrifice his only son. Our Sages, of blessed memory, teach us that Avraham Avinu was willing to go to any length to teach us to do a mitzvah."

"So what does that have to do with the 'God Box'?"

"It's that when I love something very dearly, I'm willing to release it to God."

My mind's on my mother, ill in Los Angeles.

God, please, I'm thinking. *Let me get it, too*. The cold air hits, I climb into the cab, and Ahuvah Gray calls out, "*L'hitraot!*" and disappears upstairs.

Sarah Shapiro lives in Jerusalem and writes for various publications in Israel and the United States. She is the author of *Growing with My Children, Don't You Know*

It's a Perfect World, and *A Gift Passed Along: A Woman Looks at the World Around Her.* She edited the ArtScroll anthology *Of Home and Heart* and the *Our Lives* anthology series, of which Volume III, *The Mother in Our Lives*, is forthcoming.

Reaching Out

Chapter One

The Returning of a Lost Object: Shira's Story

I n September 2000, the Palestinian Arabs renewed the violence of the Intifada, exploding with their bombs and bullets our attempt to live and grow in our holy land in peace. Distraught but not despairing, I gathered all my strength and focused on the book of *Tehillim*. The first psalm especially comforted me because it describes man as a tree planted by the rivers of water and bringing forth fruit in God's season. Surely this was the season for me to anchor myself to the teachings found in the Psalms.

The beautiful symphony that sprang up in my soul from the *Tehillim* seemed to silence the noise of the shrapnel and strengthen my resolve to pray and to increase my love for Eretz Yisrael.

In December, though, a few months after the breakout of violence, I felt that the more I prayed, the more intense the suicide bombings seemed to become. My prayers didn't seem to be helping at all. I was exhausted, traumatized by each fatal attack, but dutifully I continued to pray. My grandmother had taught me from an early age about the efficacy of prayer; I would not allow the shattered fragments of a blown-up bus to shatter my belief in the value of prayer.

Just when I thought I had no strength left, I was called to lecture at the Aish HaTorah Fellowships Program. Despite the ongoing violence, a number of irreligious young women would be arriving within a few weeks from South Africa and Australia to spend Chanukah in Israel. I wanted my message to the group to be inspirational, to renew the flames of their Jewish souls as the *shamash* lights the flames of the rest of the menorah. Perhaps it would also be a cure for me, lightening the heavy burden of the daily tragedies that were crushing my spirit. But what could I possibly say that would rekindle the flames of those young girls' souls — and of my own?

Days before the lecture, my thoughts shifted from the Arab uprising to the needs of the forthcoming group. Our Sages, of blessed memory, put places in the prayer where one can pause and say a personal request. I took the opportunity and opened my heart to my Creator:

"Hashem, what are the spiritual needs of these girls? I don't consider myself a public speaker, but I know it's the younger generation that we've got to reach. Please help me touch the hearts of Your chosen people."

A verse in *Mishlei* states, "The preparation of the heart are man's, but the answer of the tongue is from God" (*Mishlei* 16:1). Rashi explains the verse this way: "The preparations of the heart are man's" — man arranges his counsel and his words in his heart. "But the answer of the tongue is from God" — the Holy One, blessed be He, can make one stumble with his words or prepare a good reply for him. The question facing me as I stood in prayer was would God cause me to stumble in my words, or would He prepare a good reply for me?

As I stood before God during *Shemoneh Esrei*, the answer came to me. "To speak into the souls of these girls, speak directly from the heart. Don't use complicated Hebrew terms. Keep the talk simple, sprinkled with humor, relying on the lessons of your past and your own pain in the present to come together with a message that will show these girls hope for their future."

Sometimes, in moments of silent prayer, my soul receives a kind of elevation, a sort of spiritual fine tuning. As mind, heart, and soul came together in my moment of prayer, my thoughts began to arrange themselves with little effort on my part; God's reply began to form in my mind.

Several days later, I entered a room in the Old City. The group was small, but the atmosphere of sincere anticipation filled the room. At a time when tourists and students were canceling their trips to the country, these girls had come to find meaning to their Jewishness. Would my words help them in their search?

Jeanne Rubin, a South African staff member of Aish HaTorah, introduced me. During her speech, I thought, *They are very courageous to come to Eretz Yisrael at a time like this. Kol hakavod to them.*

During my lecture my attention was caught by a lovely girl seated in the front row. As I began my speech, she started to cry. As others laughed at my anecdotes, her eyes filled with tears. What inner turmoil had my simple words aroused?

At the conclusion of the lecture the participants eagerly voiced their questions about my motivation for becoming a Jew. They also wanted my advice on how to handle their parents' questions or objections to their own new religious convictions. "How do I tell my parents that I want to observe Shabbos?" "Do I have to stop wearing pants and cover my elbows?" "How many times do I have to pray each day?" "Can I eat in my mother's nonkosher kitchen?"

I answered their excited questions with advice and anecdotes that I had learned from the rabbis and *rebbetzins* in seminary. The atmosphere was light and enthusiastic.

Suddenly, the girl with the tear-stained face made her way to the front of the crowd. Her voice trembling, she asked, "Ms. Gray, why are Orthodox Jews so insensitive? Why is it that they think the entire world has to be just like them?" Her voice got louder as she poured out a list of complaints and grievances, finishing by saying emphatically, "I was raised in a *frum* home, and I want nothing to do with Orthodox Judaism!"

I was moved by her words and deeply touched by her honesty. At that moment I just wanted to throw my arms around her and console her, but I didn't even know her name. Instead I braced myself and explained my feelings.

"How can I not love Orthodox Judaism?" I asked, hoping that my words would touch her. "If our Sages had not preserved Judaism the way it is, a person like myself would not have been able to tap into our rich spiritual heritage. Sure, we make 'fences' around the Torah; sure, we see things from the one, all-important focus of Torah. How else would Torah life have survived through generations of physical and spiritual attacks? How else would I have come home to a place I'd never been to before?"

With those words, I gave the girl my address, uncertain whether I would ever hear from her again.

When I got back to Bayit Vegan, the first person I called was Rabbi Yosef Ben Shlomo Hakohen, one of my spiritual teachers. I related everything I had felt and what had transpired at the lecture. I talked about the intimacy of the group, their sincerity and courage, and concluded, "I believe that every girl in that room is going to do *teshuvah*. In fact, the one who cried throughout the entire lecture had her *teshuvah* process start today." It was at that moment that I realized I hadn't even asked her name.

A year passed. I had completely forgotten about the lecture, as well as my conversation with Rabbi Hakohen. My first book, *My Sister, the Jew*, had finally come out. I was tremendously grateful and thankful to God. Inundated with lecture engagements and book signings, my life took a turn.

One month before my lecture tour to England and America, I received a telephone call from the secretary of Rabbi Moshe Chalkowski, head of the Mechina program at Neve Yerushalayim, asking if I was available to lecture about my book in the next few days. I hastily replied, "Yes."

Neve Yerushalayim — my alma mater! What a thrill for a former student to return to the place where she studied to share her own lessons with newer students.

Preparing for my trip, and now also considering what to say at this, perhaps my most important speaking engagement, kept me busy. It kept me so busy, in fact, that I almost didn't take the time to read a lesson that Rabbi Hakohen sent me as part of a study program. Fortunately I somehow found the time to read it.

> "One should also take note of the emphasis which the Torah places on caring for the needs of one's fellow. For example, we are forbidden to ignore another Jew's lost object. Even if the object is worth but a few cents, and even if the owner is unaware of its loss, nevertheless we are commanded to pick it up and return it to him. Now if the Torah commands us to be so concerned with our fellow's material possessions, which have value only in this temporal world, how much more must we be concerned with matters affecting his soul, which lives on eternally." (*Chofetz Chaim: A Lesson a Day* [ArtScroll/Mesorah Publications, 1995], p. 177)
>
> Just as there is a mitzvah to return to someone his lost physical possessions, so too it is a mitzvah to return to someone his lost spiritual possessions. As it is written: "The Torah that Moshe commanded us is the heritage of the Community of Jacob" (*Devarim* 33:4). If a Jew has lost his connection to this heritage, then it is a mitzvah to help him discover his lost spiritual possession.

It felt wonderful to be walking again in the halls of Neve, not a beginning student with so much to learn, but actually one with her own lesson to teach. I walked to the library/*beis midrash*, amazed that the hallways were buzzing just like the days when I was a student there. My heart leaped with joy and enthusiasm as the room began to fill up. Some of the faces looked familiar. I would be speaking in front of my own teachers, including Rabbi Brown, Rebbetzin Rothman, and Rebbetzin Heller!

I was filled with excitement. I had been trained in the art of studying an audience by scanning the faces to ascertain their reactions, and I relaxed immediately when I saw that the girls were fascinated by my story, warm and receptive to my message. The fact that I had studied in that very room for a year brought speaker and audience together in an unusual bond.

Throughout the lecture my attention was constantly drawn to the face of a beautiful girl with blonde hair and blue eyes. Where had I seen her before? I couldn't place her. Suddenly, as I spoke, her eyes filled with tears. Even while everyone else was laughing, she continued to cry.

During the question-and-answer session, my eyes kept returning to the girl with the lovely, tear-stained face.

The lecture ended, and I was immediately surrounded by girls seeking autographed copies of my book. I looked through the crowd, trying to spot that familiar, tear-stained face.

The hubbub of questions and signings continued. I was nearly out of books.

Suddenly I heard a familiar voice speaking softly with a South African accent. "Excuse me, Ahuvah, do you remember me?"

Before I raised my head, I knew it was the South African girl I had spoken to a year before — finally I could place the teary young woman. When I saw how she was dressed I couldn't believe it. She could pass the scrutiny of any *rebbetzin* — a far cry from her appearance a year before.

"What happened to you?"

"Ahuvah, I have to tell you, my life was transformed by your story that day. I went directly to my room to look up all those verses of *Tehillim* that you quoted, first in English and then in Hebrew. How much more meaningful they seemed after I heard you describe how your grandmother taught you the twenty-third psalm at four years old! I knew I had to find the God that you talked about."

I couldn't believe what my ears were hearing. By now I was almost in tears, but the other girls were getting impatient. Before she left, I told her that I had been invited to speak in South Africa. She invited me to stay with her parents.

"I would love to meet your parents. I know they were praying for you and they must be wonderful people."

Once again we exchanged e-mail addresses and she gave me her mobile telephone number. The girl's eyes were bright now, not with tears but with excitement. I felt the depth of her emotion, but the crowd around us made it impossible for her to say more. She disappeared into the throng, and I went on with the book signing.

While I was signing I remembered that I had forgotten to give her an autographed copy of my book — and that I didn't even know her name. I was determined, nevertheless, to go and find her when I finished.

A few minutes later, the last girl took a book, thanked me with a smile, and left the room. I had one book left after the book signing. Surely I would find this girl again to give it to her?

At the moment that I thought of her, she suddenly reappeared.

"Thank God, you're back," I exclaimed. "Before you disappear again — please tell me your name!"

"Shira Taylor," she replied.*

---

*   Not her real name.

"Please, please, won't you accept this copy of my book?" Shira hesitated, wanting to pay, but I insisted that she take it as a gift.

Why did it mean so much to me that I should get to know this girl, that I should know that she would read my story? Why did I insist that she accept my words as a gift?

Perhaps the answer is that somehow this young girl with the crying eyes had at that moment given me a gift of her own.

Many years before, when I was a minister, I was asked each year to fill out a questionnaire stating my goals for the coming year. Each time, I wrote the same words: "My ministry calls me to work with the Jewish people."

Once I started my travel agency specializing in group movements to Israel, I thought I had fulfilled that dream. But intuitively I knew that somewhere in the distant future I was destined for a more meaningful connection to the Jews, something new that would ignite my soul, and that something hadn't happened yet.

It hadn't happened yet, that is, until I met Shira Taylor.

For some reason, the experience of meeting Shira those two times, the knowledge that she was seeking to find something and that she was finding it through my words, my story, confirmed many unanswered questions for me. I saw the inner weaving of the threads of Divine providence in our two meetings. Hashem had picked me to become a messenger for His people. All those sleepless nights I had spent immersed in my religious studies were really part of the plan of God. Now I knew He had been directing my path every step of the way.

I took a deep breath before posing the inevitable question. "Shira, everyone in my neighborhood has been asking me if I would write a sequel to my book. If you would be kind enough to tell me in your own words what happened on that icy December morning, I will write that book."

"Ahuvah, it would be my pleasure to share with you what happened, but I am leaving for South Africa in a few days and I will have to send my story to you. I want you to know that I am now davening two times a day, *shacharis* and *minchah*, because of your story about your grandmother."

Could Shira, the girl whose name means "song," know how my own heart sang as she spoke these words? Could she even grasp how much her last statement meant to me? Who could imagine that by my sharing the story of my grandmother's life, Shira Taylor, born half a world away, brought up religious and having left the fold, would find her way back? What a *kiddush haShem*, and what a merit for my grandmother.

And what an inspiration for me.

We parted, with a promise from Shira to write me her whole story and an invitation to stay in her parents' home when I visited South Africa. I left Neve invigorated and headed for the bus to Bayit Vegan. Reciting *Tehillim* on the bus, I suddenly remembered the lesson that I had read about the returning of a lost object. This time the lost object was a Jewish *neshamah*. And I had had the *zechus*, the merit, to return it!

When I returned home, the first thing I did was call Rabbi Hakohen to let him know how well the lesson had been learned by me today.

"Ahuvah, do you mean to tell me it's the same girl that you told me about? Don't you remember that you said you believed every girl in that room was going to do *teshuvah*, especially the one from South Africa?" Only then did I remember that I had shared the entire story with Rabbi Hakohen the year before.

"Ahuvah, there's a *midrash* that states: 'Every person that you bring under the *Shechinah* is considered one that you gave birth to.' I believe you're going to have many more of these experiences."

I had returned Shira to her lost heritage — and she had helped me find my own mission!

Erev Rosh HaShanah. Almost a year since the beginning of the Intifada. It was a time for introspection, a day for quiet, intense soul searching. I looked back at the difficult year behind and forward with trust and faith to the year ahead.

It was on this day that I received the gift of Shira's words over e-mail, like a *bas kol* come to strengthen me for the new year.

This was Shira's e-mail:

In December 2000, I sat in a crowded room in the Old City of Jerusalem awaiting a speaker. I was on an Aish HaTorah program along with fourteen other girls from South Africa and Australia. The program, called "Fellowships," was intended to educate young women about Judaism, to prove God's existence and to create a foundation for future spiritual growth. Unlike the other girls in the program, who had very little or no religious background, I was raised in a frum home.

The truth is that, despite my background, I was apathetic, complacent, and totally missing the point. I had somehow missed out on one vital component of being Jewish. A fundamental truth had somehow never made it into my religious schooling (perhaps because I had cut so many classes). I did not grasp the concept that God loved me. I didn't know that my purpose in this world is to develop a relation-ship with Him. I had kept twenty-one years of Shabbosim, main-tained some semblance of observant life, and was considered by those who knew me to be religious. But I had no idea that this concept of a relationship with God was not something that was abstract, but could be taken literally.

From about the age of eighteen, I had unconcernedly watched as my Judaism gradually dwindled to a shadow of what it had once been (which was not much); I stopped keeping kosher and learned ab-solutely no Torah. I had the ridiculous impression that I had heard it all before. I did, however, feel quite spiritual. It was the kind of spirituality that was somewhat external. I saw God in the trees, the flowers, and the hills — in sunlight glittering off vast stretches of wa-ter. I saw God everywhere except in me. The God of Torah was a co-lossal Creator who had made heaven and earth, taken the Jews out of Egypt, laid down the law, and proceeded to observe His creations, now and then tinkering with massive events in history but not with me or with my life.

And then on that ordinary winter's day, in that tiny room over-looking a children's play yard in the Jewish Quarter, in walked Ahuvah Gray. She instantly struck me as being one of the most beautiful women I had ever seen. It seemed that her soul shone through her eyes and illuminated her skin. I sat and listened to her story in awe at what she had found...a relationship with Hashem. She saw Him in her life at every step.

I can attempt to dissect the rational reasons for her profound im-pact on my life, but to be honest I believe it was simply a resonance, a soul connection, a miracle. I cried for a solid hour. While my friends laughed at her hilarious anecdotes, my soul rose and fell with her journey. While everyone in the room listened with fascination to her adventurous path to Torah and Judaism, my soul wept.

I had been oblivious to this dimension of living. I, who had been handed the Torah on a silver platter with an excellent Jewish education, a family immersed in Torah life, and parents who were so trusting, patient, and giving. I wept for the lost years where I had been frozen and closed and ignorant. I wept because Ahuvah had fought so hard and with such love and joy for what I had always dismissed.

As Ahuvah described how her Baptist grandmother had taught her the Tehillim and how they whispered to her in times of joy and desperation and formed the narration to her struggles and triumphs, I wept. I had barely bothered to read their English translation. Ahuvah described how she had bought a siddur and read the entire thing, devouring its inspirational truths and praying from it three times daily, and I cried bitter tears at how I had considered those ancient prayers as irrelevant, remote, and inapplicable. Ahuvah had seen the beauty of my own religion, while for years I had only yawned.

I felt ashamed and small but also filled with an immense desire to find what she had found. I wanted to feel what she felt. I can only describe my awakening as a miracle because Hashem opened my heart that day. Ahuvah's beautiful neshamah had brought light and hope to my spiritual journey. From that day I began to read the prayers, first in English and then in Hebrew; I began to read Tehillim and learn some commentaries and I started to read Pirkei Avos. I wanted to make my heritage my own. Today I daven every morning, say berachos again on food, keep kosher, and say Shema twice a day, and I am committed to living a Torah life. There are no doubts in my mind that my spiritual growth was catalyzed by my davening, which, in turn, was inspired by Ahuvah.

The Tehillim now narrate my growth and pain, my sadness and joy, just as Ahuvah described. Through davening I now talk to Hashem, my Creator. I say "please" and "thank you," I ask questions. I tell Him when I'm frightened, angry, or hopeless. I tell Him when I feel alone, when I feel full, when I feel loved and happy and safe. I talk to Hashem all the time.

Often as I'm about to daven or say Tehillim, I think of that beautiful woman who traveled from Chicago to Los Angeles and literally all over the world. Finally, after fourteen trips to Israel, which is now her home, she came to stand in front of me on an icy December morning to announce to my soul that prayer is everything. She passed on a message begun by her Baptist grandmother and reinforced by her teachers in Jerusalem. This message profoundly changed my life and continues to do so as I share it with others.

There is a concept in Judaism that the merit of observing mitzvos and doing good deeds goes both to the doer and to the person who inspired those actions. At 120 Ahuvah will have lived a relatively short time as a Jew, having converted at age fifty-one. But she will also have lived many lifetimes as a Torah-observant Jew, as the merits of the mitzvos of the people she has inspired mount. Ahuvah can consider all the years of Torah growth ahead of me as her own.

I thank Hashem for placing me in that room on that day and for opening my heart to the glittering treasures of Tehillim and tefillah as experienced by Ahuvah.

When I first met Shira, she was crying. When I finished reading Shira's words, I was the one in tears. Her words pierced my heart, just as mine had pierced hers. I thought, *Hashem, she will write her own book one day.* Perhaps she would give me a gift of her book, as I had given her mine!

I couldn't go into the Jewish New Year without reading her

story to Rabbi Hakohen.

Oh, how true his words were. "Ahuvah, every person that you bring under the *Shechinah* is considered one that you gave birth to."

That was one of the most wonderful Rosh HaShanahs I had ever experienced.

Despite all the horrendous events of the past year, I was able to enter the shul *erev Rosh HaShanah* knowing that Hashem was working His plan into my life. Deep inside I knew it was the will of God for Shira's *neshamah* to make peace with her Maker, and for me to get the message of this peace on this special *erev Rosh HaShanah*.

Chapter Two

An Appointed Place for an Appointed Purpose

One *erev Shabbos*, as I did my chores, I hummed to myself as I reflected on the events of the week.

Several days before, during the spontaneous part of *Shemoneh Esrei*, I had davened for *parnasah*, for a good and honorable income. As soon as I finished the silent prayer, the telephone rang. Chani G., program coordinator at Me'ohr Bais Yaakov, was on the phone. As she began to speak, I thought about the *passuk* in *Yirmiyahu* that says, "Call to Me and I will answer you; and I will tell you great and mighty things that you do not know" (*Yirmiyahu* 33:3).

"Hello, Ahuvah, I apologize for calling you on such short notice, but I am ill and was wondering if you could speak at our seminary tonight."

I accepted without hesitation. In my opinion she wasn't calling on short notice at all; everything was happening in exactly the right time.

"Chani, it's my pleasure. I would love to lecture to the girls tonight."

Me'ohr Bais Yaakov, a one-year seminary program under the auspices of Neve Yerushalayim for eighteen-year-old girls from religious backgrounds, is located in Bayit Vegan. Chani asked me to be there at 8:15 p.m.

Half an hour later, the telephone rang once again with yet another answer to my prayer for *parnasah*. It was an invitation from Rabbi Yechezkel Fox to lecture in Zichron Yaakov as well. Now my heart was fueled with gratitude to Hashem for having heard my prayers and giving an answer so quickly.

The rest of the day passed quickly, and before I realized it I was scurrying to grab a few books to take with me for the lecture. I walked down Bayit Vegan Street to the seminary, enjoying the lovely spring breeze in the air. I had no idea what I was going to say, but I knew that Hashem, who provided me with *parnasah* that I needed, would also give me the words to inspire my listeners' hearts.

The girls had already begun to assemble when I arrived at the school. As always, I marveled at how they stood up when I walked in the room. It always made me chuckle a bit inside — why were they standing up for me? If it was for Rebbetzin Heller, well, of course I would stand with them — but standing up for me? However, I knew this was a part of their upbringing and character development. Good *middos* led them to show this respect for teachers — even if the teacher still wasn't sure exactly what she was going to say!

I began softly to speak about my journey and felt their rising interest. I noticed that several of the girls had brought their personal copies of my book, so they were familiar with my story.

But my spoken words seemed to have a further impact on their inquisitive souls.

While I was speaking, I sensed the girls' genuine concern about the current events. What could I say to help allay their fear, to help them deal with the traumas that we had all been sharing for much too long?

I had once read in *Mishlei* that "a glad heart cheers the face" (*Mishlei* 15:13). As I told my story, I mingled humor with the unusual facts. Since most of the men in Bayit Vegan dress in black, I explained that I felt comfortable living there because I had moved from one Black neighborhood to another. The girls, so full of anxiety and fear before I began speaking, shook with healing laughter.

During the question-and-answer period, the depth of the girls' fear and pain came clear.

The first girl asked, "We know Hashem is running the world, but all the daily suffering of our people causes us so much pain. What can we do to make the situation better?" Another girl asked, "What can we do to make our lives safer?" Perhaps the most poignant question came from a quiet voice in the back of the room. "Doesn't Hashem hear our *tefillos*?"

I held my breath for a moment, silently praying that my words would have the power to heal.

"Those are all good questions. We definitely know that Hashem is running the world. Yes, He hears our *tefillos* no matter what and even though He doesn't always answer us immediately, He does answer when we merit it. It is written that a person who speaks slander and evil gossip defiles his mouth to such a degree that his prayers are not accepted. 'Life and death are in the hands of the tongue!' That is why it is so important to watch what we say. Each individual has to examine himself and be honest with his *tefillos* and to do *teshuvah* in the specific area where it is needed. And the gates of tears are always open. When all the other gates are closed, we have to cry out to Hashem in sincerity. Then, if we merit it, the redemption will come!"

Wanting to end on a positive note, I asked the girls' permission to close out with a brief story, even though the class period had ended.

The girls listened in rapt attention as I told the story of Shira Taylor. In my heart, I asked Hashem to help me to communicate strength and hope to these precious girls. This was not the first time I had shared Shira's story with others. Listeners were always moved when I described Shira's letter and how she had been inspired to return to Torah observance.

At the conclusion of the lecture, I noticed that a few girls were teary eyed. Grasping the moment, I asked for a volunteer to read Shira's entire e-mail. The girls all turned to face one of their friends. Leah should read it, they insisted — after all, she's South African!

As Leah started to read Shira's e-mail with her distinctive South African accent, she brought us all to tears. For the girls, it was a chance to hear the story of true *teshuvah*. For me, I could almost hear Shira's voice again — her accent, her words, and the depth of her emotion.

When she finished one of the girls asked, "Can we sing you a song?" And they sang:

> *Elokei avi ve'aromemeihu* — The God of my father, and I will
> exalt Him,

Ani malkah bas melachim — I am a queen, the daughter of kings,

Ahuvah bas ahuvim — Beloved, the daughter of beloved ones,

Kedoshah bas kedoshim — Holy, the daughter of holy ones,

Tehorah bas tehorim — Pure, the daughter of the pure ones.

When they finished the song, I knew their hearts had been touched just as mine had been. One of the girls said, "Ahuvah, we've never sung that song with such passion before. You really touched our hearts tonight."

I was very moved by their comments and especially pleased when two of the girls volunteered to make me a copy of the tape of my lecture and the song.

Words inspire songs, and songs inspire words. The following *erev Shabbos*, I wrote a lengthy e-mail to Shira in South Africa: "You can't imagine the impact your story is having on seminary girls, all because you were honest and shared with us the innermost thoughts of your heart."

When I finished the e-mail, the doorbell rang. To my surprise, it was the girls from Me'ohr Bais Yaakov. I thanked them for the tape and once again listened to the words of that beautiful song.

The whole sequence of events was so amazing. I couldn't stop thinking about it as I went about my chores.

That Shabbos was *Parashas Emor*. In *Vayikra* 23, Hashem describes to Moshe the special days in the Jewish calender: Shabbos and the festival days. The Hebrew word for "festivals" is *moadim* — appointed times. More specifically, festivals are the special days when we, the Jewish people, relinquish our daily activities and meet with God.

Rabbi Samson Raphael Hirsch in *Horeb*, ch. 23, explains it this way: "*Moadim*, appointed seasons, summon us to submit ourselves entirely to the contemplation and inner realization of those ideals which lie at their foundation. Just as *moed* in space refers to the locality which men have as their appointed place of assembly for an appointed purpose — such as the *Ohel Moed*, the Tent of Meeting, so *moed* in time is a point in time which summons us communally to an appointed activity — in this case an inner activity. Thus *moadim* are the days which stand out from the other days of the year. They summon us from our everyday life to halt and to dedicate all our spiritual activities to them."

I realized that Shira Taylor and I had experienced a "personal *moed*," in time and in place, arranged by Hashem. He had brought us together on that cold December day to that room in Jerusalem's Old City. The words of the Me'ohr girls' song expressed what had transpired in Shira's life at that appointed time and place. Hashem had prepared her soul to receive, just like He had prepared the hearts of all of us to receive the Torah at Har Sinai.

I lit my Shabbos candles with a joyful heart, grateful for the privilege of sharing my story with such wonderful young people.

That Shabbos, I was set to eat lunch at the home of Yehudis and Don Mishell. I had met the Mishells two years prior. Yehudis is a psychologist, a teacher, and the author of *Beyond Your Ego* (Lakewood, NJ: CIS Publishers, 1991). Her husband, Don, is a legal recruiter.

That meal was more than a Shabbos lunch meal. It became a *moed* — "an appointed place for an appointed purpose" — for all of those present.

When I knocked on the Mishells' door the following day, Don opened the door with a hearty "Good Shabbos." Yehudis was in the kitchen with Rena, a student whom I had met before. Another student, a woman from Har Nof, and I were introduced as Yehudis and Rena joined us in the living room. Shortly afterwards Rabbi Hakohen arrived and introductions were made once again. The Mishells were expecting three other girls, but we started the meal because the hour was getting late.

After Kiddush and washing our hands, we sat down to a lovely array of salads, baked salmon, and Don's homemade pickles. Our conversation was lively and relaxing. I felt very much at ease in the Mishells' home, thanks to the warm, congenial atmosphere and Don's deep thoughts on the Torah portion.

Yehudis asked me in her usual gracious way, "Ahuvah, where will you be off globe-trotting to in the near future?"

"Hong Kong, Australia, and South Africa," I replied.

Rabbi Hakohen, who never misses a beat, said, "Ahuvah, have you ever told them your experience with the girl from South Africa?"

"Not to my recollection," I replied, and so I launched into what had gradually become one of my favorite stories.

When I finished, Yehudis was teary eyed. Don and the other guests were listening attentively. I closed by saying how excited I was about being a guest in the home of Shira's parents. What would they be like, I wondered. How would they feel meeting me — the woman whose early memory of my grandmother had returned their daughter to them?

"Can you imagine what it's like to have this kind of drama pending for eighteen months?" I said to everyone.

One of Yehudis's guests, Freida Leah Cohen, said, "Ahuvah, I was at that lecture at Neve that day when Shira Taylor was present. You truly have an extremely inspirational story. I was very touched by it as well. It's lovely to hear this dimension."

Just before we started the main course, there was a knock at the door and the three additional guests arrived. They had already heard Kiddush, so Yehudis and Don had them wash and sit down to join the rest of the group.

When Yehudis introduced the girls, Rabbi Hakohen spoke up. "Ahuvah, since two of the girls are from South Africa, you must tell that story again."

I sat there hesitantly, not wanting to monopolize the conversation. "Why don't you tell them?"

Then the girl sitting right next to me exclaimed, "Wait a minute, are you Ahuvah Gray? You know my sister."

"Who is your sister?"

"Shira Taylor!"

At first there was complete, stunned silence. I didn't know whether to laugh or cry. We all sat there astounded, because we knew that this was *yad Hashem*, the hand of God. It was an extension of my personal *moed* with Shira Taylor.

Shira's sister and I embraced while everyone was sitting as though it was a scene from a movie. The other girl from South Africa said, "Wait a minute. Are you the lady who used to be a minister and became an Orthodox Jew?"

"Yes."

"You're the reason I am learning at Neve. My neighbor in Cape Town told me your story and I was so moved I wanted to study Torah in Jerusalem."

I was speechless. A chapter of *Tehillim* sprang up in my soul: "My Lord, You have been an abode for us in all generations.... Teach us to count our days, then we shall acquire a heart of wisdom.... May the pleasantness of my Lord, our God, be upon us — our handiwork, establish for us; our handiwork, establish it" (*Tehillim*, ch. 90). At that moment, I felt that I could see the fulfillment of Hashem's plan as it was unfolding in my life.

It was as though Hashem had orchestrated all those events so that the story would be imprinted on our *neshamos*. I was beginning to see it as a template for the *teshuvah* process of future generations.

As we started the main course, I told the story about Shira Taylor once again. I had to speak succinctly because I felt sapped of strength by the surprises and emotions of that Shabbos meal. Thank goodness, Yehudis's *cholent* gave me my much-needed refreshment!

As I watched Shira's sister listening to my story, laughing and crying simultaneously, in my mind's eye I was transported to the tent of Sarah Imeinu. I remembered how the Midrash (*Bereishis Rabbah* 60:16) states that her Shabbos lamp burned continuously from Shabbos to Shabbos. I remembered the words of that beautiful song, "*Elokei avi ve'aromemeihu; ani malkah bas melachim* — The God of my father, and I will exalt Him; I am a queen, the daughter of kings," that the girls had sung to me after hearing Shira's story. Shira had said it in her own words: "I can only describe my awakening as a miracle because Hashem opened my heart that day."

At one point in the story her sister leaned over and said, "Ahuvah, you forgot to tell them that Shira was apprehensive about coming over to you at the lecture because she is very shy."

Grateful and humbled that she had brought me back to the table and away from the "tent," I continued my story. I had no idea what was going to unfold next. In all honesty I felt like I was completely out of the picture and Hashem was using my vocal cords to express His will.

When I reached the point in the story when Shira came over to me at the end of the lecture, in my mind's eye I returned to Sarah's tent. I remembered the commentary of the Tiferes Tzion, a twentieth century sage of Jerusalem, that the doors of the tent were opened wide, indicating her generosity, and because of the blessing on her challahs, Sarah had food to feed all her guests. I felt like it was in the merit of Sarah that we were all present at the Mishells' Shabbos table together, eating together, blessed as our hearts opened up to one another.

Walking home, I felt weak, sapped of strength, as if I had just given two lectures in a two-hour period. But when I hummed the beautiful melody of that song, it gave me new strength with each step I took.

There were three weeks left before my departure to Hong Kong, Australia, and South Africa. When Shabbos was over, I had lots to do before I could go to sleep. When I looked at the clock it was 1:00 a.m. I tried to settle down, but the events of the Shabbos meal made me feel too excited.

I finally fell asleep, but only after a *passuk* from *Yeshayah* that

somehow encapsulated what that Shabbos ignited within me
on a spiritual level came to my mind:

> Look at the rock whence you were dug.... Look at Avraham,
> your father, and Sarah, who bore you....
>
> *(Yeshayah 5:1–2)*

Round the World

Chapter Three

Hong Kong

he Orient. A land of mystery, of exotic scents and spices, of delicate art, or, more mundanely, a land that is today one of the largest commercial centers of the world. Yet it is a land that, in all my world travels, I had never felt a desire to visit. The Far East might have its fascination for some, but it simply didn't attract me. Despite my background in business and marketing, I ignored the news about the rise and fall of the stock exchange and the bullish or bearish fate of China and Japan, the international leaders in the automotive and telecommunications industry.

I was therefore somewhat hesitant when my travel agent, Yisrael Meir Friedman, suggested I speak in Hong Kong. He had just finished booking my ticket for Australia and South Africa, and he said, "Ahuvah, you have a stopover in Hong Kong. Why don't you do a lecture there?"

"Thank you, but I'm not really drawn to the Far East. Their culture is foreign to me, and besides, I don't know anyone there."

"There's a Jewish community there, you know. If you are there already, Ahuvah, you have a responsibility to your readership. Call Avraham Schwartzbaum, maybe he can suggest some contacts."

When I hung up the telephone his words lingered in my mind like an echo from the past.

Responsibility and *commitment* were words I grew up with. I recalled the warm memories of my maternal grandfather, who was my hero at the tender age of four. He used to pick me up to his knee and say, "My word is my bond. Little Delores, if a person can't depend upon your word it means that you are not trustworthy. It represents a lack of responsibility."

Responsibility.... The word stared me in the face. I heard my granddaddy's voice.... "Little Delores, I want you to learn to be a responsible person."

Reluctantly, I called Dr. Avraham Schwartzbaum, author of *The Bamboo Cradle* (Feldheim Publishers, 1988), a neighbor of mine in Bayit Vegan. Dr. Schwartzbaum said that he had lectured for Rabbi Mordechai Avtzon in Hong Kong and assured me that he felt his community would benefit from hearing my story. When I hung up the telephone there was this huge smile on my face, and I sensed that my granddaddy was watching me from somewhere up there — and that some time in the near future, he would be watching me in Hong Kong.

After sending an e-mail to Rabbi Avtzon, I checked with the volunteer team in Melbourne, Australia, which was organizing the lecture tour. It turned out that the head of the committee, Samuel Roden, knew Rabbi Avtzon, and he arranged for me to spend a Shabbos in Hong Kong. I was scheduled to speak on Friday night in their shul.

The next day, when I looked at the calendar to check the date of my departure, I couldn't believe my eyes. I was scheduled to depart for Hong Kong on *erev Tishah B'Av*. I froze. I had been living in Eretz Yisrael for seven years and had never been outside the country for any major fast days or holidays. To commemorate the terrible loss of our nation as I was leaving Eretz Yisrael — how could I endure it?

I could not imagine spending Tishah B'Av far away from home, not sitting on the floor of my shul in Yerushalayim, not sitting next to my *rebbetzin* as I heard the mournful chanting of *Megillas Eichah*.

With my next breath I called my *abba*, Rabbi Heyman, the rabbi of HaGra shul in Bayit Vegan, to ask a *she'eilah*. Should I leave Eretz Yisrael at such a significant time? On the other hand, could I postpone a lecture tour that was already booked and would give me the opportunity to bring my message to the farthest corners of the world?

Rabbi Heyman listened carefully and stated that my concerns were valid, especially with the current situation — the *"matzav,"* as it is known in Israel. He advised me to speak with Rabbi Yosef Shalom Elyashiv and call him back with his reply. Rebbetzin Heyman later explained to me that he felt it was a tremendous responsibility to rule on such a question and he felt that I should ask a *gadol*. Like my grandfather, Rabbi Heyman took his responsibilities seriously.

Rabbi Elyashiv's reply was that I should by all means proceed with my travel plans because it was a mitzvah and a *kiddush haShem*. He also gave me a *berachah* that I should be successful and go in peace and return in peace.

I called Rabbi Heyman the next morning to give him the

news. Having anticipated the answer to my *she'eilah*, he had already checked the halachos regarding fasting under such conditions as well as fasting in different time zones. He told me what time I should start my fast and what time it should end. This was going to be a first. In all my years of traveling, I had never been on an airplane during a fast. *May Hashem give me strength!* I thought.

I wrote down everything that Rabbi Heyman advised me to do according to halachah. I could take eight drops of water within an hourly period if I felt faint, since an ill person is exempt from fasting.

When we ended the conversation Rabbi Heyman said, "Ahuvah, this is a tremendous responsibility that Hashem has given you. You should be *matzliach!*"

There was that word again! Now, with all the travel aspects of the trip resolved, I had to settle down and focus on the spiritual ramifications of being outside of Eretz Yisrael for a major fast.

As I started packing, my mind turned to my first Tishah B'Av in Eretz Yisrael. I was studying at Ulpan Akiva, and it was there that I received my first ephemeral feeling that I was a Jew with a Jewish *neshamah*. It was just a beginning, but it was enough to make me take on my first fast — Tishah B'Av. This year, the fast would find me far from the land of my people — but closer to my people than ever before.

I recalled the beautiful words of *Yeshayah*: "Come, let us go up to the Lord's mount, to the house of the God of Jacob, and let Him teach us of His ways, and we will go in His paths, for out of Zion shall the Torah come forth, and the word of the Lord from Jerusalem" (*Yeshayah* 2:3). The latter part of the *passuk* reverberated in my ears — "For out of Zion shall the To-rah come forth and the word of the Lord from Jerusalem." My own trip, taking me out of Jerusalem at a time so close to Tishah B'Av, made me feel part of the fulfillment of that wondrous prophecy of *nechamah*, comfort.

The day of my departure, Ezra, my cab driver, arrived about twenty minutes ahead of schedule. Frantically, I grabbed my last items, pushing them into my carry-on bag.

Once we were well on our way, I realized that I had forgotten my *Tehillim*. Thank God, I knew most of the chapters by heart. As I relaxed and peered through the window at the scenery, I knew that the Master Travel Agent had overridden my personal considerations and was leading me to Hong Kong!

Once aboard the airplane, I fastened my seat belt and peered out the window during takeoff. The plane's engines roared into high gear, and we were airborne at last.

The sunlight slanted through the white clouds, sparkling against the background of blue sky. For a moment, I closed my eyes and took a deep breath. This was my first flight fasting and I wasn't quite sure of what my level of endurance would be. To take my mind off the fasting, I thought about the words of Yisrael Meir Friedman, my travel agent: "Ahuvah, you have a responsibility to your readership."

I had heard an amazing story about a Shinto priest from Rabbi David Zeller when I was a guest at his Shabbos table in Efrat. Rabbi Zeller related how a meeting with a Shinto priest had given him new motivation to seek out his own heritage and Jewish faith. Here is the story, in his own words.

"One summer, driving on my way to the annual conference of

the Association of Humanistic Psychology in New Orleans, I stopped in Arizona to visit a Japanese Shinto priest who was also a master of acupuncture. From a nearby rest stop, I called the priest, hoping that he would be available for a spontaneous visit.

"To my relief and delight, he warmly replied, 'Welcome, David. Come right over.'

"After we introduced ourselves, he looked at me with his direct gaze and asked, 'David, are you Jewish?' I was not Orthodox at the time, but mentioned that I had lived in Israel for two years before living in India as an ascetic monk, called a sadhu, for a year.

"The priest said that in the oral tradition of his Shinto religion there was an interesting story about the Jews. 'David, do you know what is oral tradition?' he asked. I assured him I knew what oral tradition meant. And this is what he told me:

"*According to the Shinto oral tradition, there had been a meeting of great spiritual teachers several thousand years ago to report on the progress of their mission: Had they succeeded in leading various peoples around the world to a spiritual awakening and evolution? Many reported of their success — from the wisdom of the Vedas in India, to the Tao in China, to the Aztec civilization in South America. Everyone felt quite good and was feeling their assignment was completed. But one person raised a troubling question.*

" '*Wasn't our mission to lead people through a material awakening and evolution and a spiritual awakening and evolution and then to bring the two together? If it was just a spiritual process, what need is there for coming into this material world? Our task was to bring the two — material and spiritual — together.*'

" '*You're right,' said the group's leader. 'We must first lead people through a material awakening and evolution, and then the spiritual*

one, and then unite them. But who amongst you will take this on?' No
one wanted that responsibility. These were all enlightened people, and
they knew that material development could only be reached by going
through possessiveness, competition, aggression, violence, and war — no
one wanted that on his shoulders. 'No volunteers?' asked the leader.
'Then I'll have to choose someone.'

"So the 'chosen people' were the Jews.

"From then on, all other spiritual traditions were split between the*
exoteric and the esoteric — the mundane and the secret — religious
dogma and spiritual experience. For if people other than the Jews knew
the spiritual reality, they would not have the motivation to develop the
material for this even higher synthesis.

"The tablets of the Ten Commandments became the Jews' symbol of*
synthesis: Spirit inscribed in Stone, spirit in matter.

"Finishing this part of the tale, the Shinto priest said to me,
'You know, in Shinto tradition we learn we have five energy
centers in our body. One center corresponds to lowest part of
back, the second is a bit higher, the third is at heart, the fourth
at throat, and the fifth at forehead. They represent levels of
conscious development and mastery. Each one has sound, like
vowel, associated with it. The lowest part has the sound *ah*, the
next level *oh*, the heart is *oo*, the throat *ay*, and the forehead *ee*.
In ancient Japan, samurai — martial artists — added the sound
of the energy center to the end of their title. This showed the
level they mastered."

" 'But in ancient Japan,' the Shinto priest told me, 'the word
for samurai was *mosh*. So if one was just beginning and had only
mastered the lowest center, one was called "Mosh-*ah*." One
who reached the level of control of the next power center was
called "Mosh-*oh*." Mastery of the heart, the emotional center,

was a "Mosh-*oo*." Mastery of the intellectual center, of speech and expression, was called "Mosh-*ay*."

" 'You know, Mosh-ay is Hebrew for Moses!' my Shinto priest exclaimed. 'Moses was on that high level to bring down the tablets of spirit in matter and to teach — give expression — to all God's instructions.' (He didn't say the following, but it occurred to me that the next level, of the forehead, the spiritual level, would be 'Mosh-ee' — which would be the level of 'Mosh-ee-ach,' Mashiach, the Messiah!)

"He went on to explain, very excitedly, that if you bring the energy down from the highest center to the lowest and back up again to the highest, going through the sounds of each center: *ee-ay-oo-oh-ah-oh-oo-ay-ee* (or something like that, but be careful) — you get the sound of the Four-Letter Name of God, the Tetragrammaton. I explained to him that in our Jewish tradition, we were not allowed to pronounce that name.

"Then he continued his story. 'Jews did a wonderful job developing the material. Wonderful job! But they forgot about the spiritual and to unite them together. And if you don't bring the spiritual and the material together — the whole world is going to blow up! I don't care, I'm ready to go!' The Shinto priest laughed, almost falling off his meditation pillow. 'My job is just to remind the Jews what their job is.'

"I sat there, quite stunned by this story and its message. But I'd been around the world and studied many of the world traditions. I said, 'That's very well and good, but the Jews aren't the only people worried about the future and its dire consequences. The Hopi Indians have a similar message, saying if people don't get their spirit and matter together, "purification day" is coming and everything will burn.'

"He replied, 'Hopi people wonderful people. Hopi religion wonderful religion. But Hopi not responsible for whole world. Jews responsible for whole world.'

"I said, 'The Buddhists speak about the end of days, and the coming of "Avalokateshwara," and that we must achieve higher states of Being.'

" 'Buddhist people wonderful people. Buddhist religion wonderful religion. But Buddhists not responsible for whole world. Jews responsible for whole world.'

"I went through Christianity, Islam, and any others that I knew. To each he answered, 'Wonderful people, wonderful religion. But not responsible for whole world. Jews responsible for whole world.'

"I came away with a new understanding of the commandments and a new appreciation for Judaism, as quite unique from many other religions, in insisting on living in the material world and in the spiritual world. No monasteries. No retreating from the world. Rather a day-to-day practice filled with practices to unite each material act with spiritual intention. The word *mitzvah*, usually translated as 'commandment,' can also be translated 'to join together.' We are 'enjoined' to live in such a way as to constantly join together heaven and earth, spirit and matter.

"No retreat? I must correct myself. Judaism gives us a spiritual retreat once a week in the Sabbath. Six days a week, we work to bring an aspect of the spiritual into the everyday material. One day a week, we strive to bring the material into the spiritual. In between our spiritual activities of prayers, rituals, and ceremonies we have the material through meals (though all cooking is completed before the Sabbath begins) — that are uplifted through inspirational learning and song.

"If the Ten Commandments (Enjoinments) are spirit in matter, then our Sabbath is matter in spirit. Our lives are balanced.

"Last but not least I must testify to God's great compassion. Had I heard this teaching of the Jews' responsibility for the world from a Jew, let alone a rabbi — I would have stood up and not so politely told him what I thought of his 'chosen people' ideas and walked out. But God, the Compassionate One, sent me the Shinto priest instead. From him I could hear it. I owe a great deal to my Jewish teachers and rebbes for helping me become who I am today, but I also owe a great deal to my Shinto priest and, needless to say, deep gratitude to the Holy Blessed One."

The phrase "Jews responsible for whole world" echoed within me. I reflected on how amazing it was that Hashem orchestrates our individual roles in being responsible. And now here I was, on Tishah B'Av, on my way to Hong Kong and beyond, to be responsible for — what? I prayed that I would find my mission and fulfill my own responsibilities to my people and the whole world fully.

Chapter Four

Jews Responsible for the Whole World

I still had a few hours left until the plane arrived in Hong Kong. My mind turned to the community there and to Rabbi Mordechai Avtzon, the rabbi in Hong Kong in whose home I would be staying. I had spent the Shabbos prior to my departure with Edi and Delia Jaeger. The Jaegers had recently made aliyah and moved to Bayit Vegan. When I mentioned to Edi that I was going to Hong Kong, his immediate reply was "You will probably meet Rabbi Mordechai Avtzon. Please give him and his wife my regards."

Edi's business necessitated that he visit Hong Kong several times a year. He had first met Rabbi Avtzon in 1985, when the rabbi was still unmarried and had recently been appointed rabbi of Ohel Leah, the only shul in Hong Kong at that time.

The shul was built by the Sassoon family from India in honor of their beloved mother, Leah Sassoon. Later, I discovered that a member of E. D. Sassoon & Co. laid the foundation stone on August 7, 1901. I was fascinated by the story because I was a frequent guest of Rabbi David Sassoon and his family in Bayit Vegan.

Some time ago, the directors of Ohel Leah had advertised for a rabbi, but received minimal response. Chabad tried to help by sending yeshivah students to minister to the needs of the community. One of these was Rabbi Avtzon. The directors asked him to accept a one-year contract to serve as the Ohel Leah rabbi, and he accepted the challenge and the responsibility.

After several months in the position, Rabbi Avtzon returned to America and married Goldie, the daughter of a well-known Lubavitch family. Her father is the Lubavitch representative in the White House and her brothers are in *shelichus*. Mordechai, for his part, comes from a family of more than ten children, and his late mother was a seventh-generation descendant of chassidim of the Baal Shem Tov.

At the end of his one-year contract, Mordechai and Goldie stayed on in Hong Kong to start their own shul at the request of the Lubavitcher rebbe, *z"l*. At first, they lived in a small room at the Hilton Hotel and rented another small room for the daily minyan, which even on Shabbos barely had ten people. As word of the bright young rabbi spread throughout the business world, the Avtzons needed to rent much larger rooms. The *kehillah* moved from small rented rooms to bigger ones, outgrew the bigger ones, and finally opened its own facilities, including a shul and kosher catering kitchen, to provide minyanim and food for the community and for visitors from around the world. After they became parents, Goldie started a school, which eventually was supported mainly by the Jewish community and attended by all the Jewish children in Hong Kong.

The Avtzons' influence spread from Hong Kong throughout the entire Far East; they sponsored *Shabbatonim*, guest speakers, internships, summer camps, and a biannual full color magazine entitled *L.I.F.E.* (Lubavitch in the Far East). Tradition has it that Eliyahu HaNavi visits every seder table as we read the prayer *"Shefoch Chamoscha"* on seder night. Since Rabbi Avtzon took responsibility for the Far East, Eliyahu HaNavi could take his sip of wine in places such as Katmandu and Yokohama, where the Avtzons have arranged Pesach sedarim for the many Jewish travelers and tourists.

Peering through the window of the airplane, I saw a cluster of little islands in the beautiful turquoise sea. My thoughts wandered back to the story of Rabbi Zeller and the Shinto priest. Jews are responsible for the whole world, the priest had said. Well, there was no island so small or faraway that it wasn't part of God's plan; certainly there is no Jewish *neshamah* that is so small or far away that it is not our responsibility. Rabbi Avtzon has brought this message to the far corners of the world. And here I was, on Tishah B'Av, flying eastward to join my words to his message.

One of the members of Rabbi Avtzon's community met me at the airport. We took a train and then a taxi to the Avtzons' home, where I would be staying. As I glanced out of the window of the train I noticed that all the buildings were tall and slim and everything looked immaculate.

When we arrived at the apartment, the fast was already over. Goldie was putting finishing touches on a surprise birthday party for the rabbi, with the help of two of her six children. Amidst all the preparations, I was shown to my room, where I immediately went to bed, too exhausted to even eat. I had really made it to Hong Kong!

I awoke a few hours later, disoriented. I dressed and made my way to the kitchen, had a glass of water, and sat down to break my fast. Our day of mourning had ended, and my job in the far reaches of the world was about to begin.

Guests kept arriving in the next hours. I had to go to bed before they all left because I simply couldn't stay awake any longer. But the hours I did stay up were enough for me to see for myself the *hachnasas orchim* that I had heard was a hallmark of the Avtzon home.

By the time I woke up and davened the next morning, Rabbi Avtzon and Goldie had gone to work. The maid was there to help me with breakfast. I wanted to go out for a walk, so I called Goldie, who directed me to the kosher market, located in the Jewish Community Center.

It was wonderful to go out and enjoy the fresh air. Walking down the stairs, however, proved a bit hazardous, since only half my foot fit on each stair! I certainly did not have Chinese or Japanese feet! All the buildings that I passed were new, with a simple charm and modern architectural beauty.

It was a lovely but hot day outside. Everyone I passed on the street was slender and dressed appropriately for the heat. All the women I saw reminded me of those little china dolls.

Goldie had told me that during the summer a lot of families go to America because the heat is almost unbearable. I recalled my first summer in Jerusalem, getting used to the intensity of the afternoon Jerusalem sun and the scorching heat of the occasional *chamsin*, heat wave, and I started to get a little homesick. At the moment all I wanted was a cold drink of water — preferably from the clear, flowing waters of Eretz Yisrael!

I returned to the Avtzons' and helped them prepare for Shabbos. Although I was still jet lagged and my body told me it couldn't possibly be nearing sundown, the sun and the clock said something different, and before I knew it Goldie, her daughters, and I were standing together, lighting our Shabbos candles. As I lit my candles and said my *berachah* the words came to my mind again: "But not responsible for the whole world. Jews responsible for the whole world." As I recited the prayer for the rebuilding of the Beis HaMikdash I recalled learning about the *korbanos* that are offered for the seventy nations during Sukkos. How strange that here I was, ushering in the most spiritual of days in China, a land that was far removed from my everyday experience, but one that is, indeed, one of the seventy nations for which we Jews are responsible.

As we were walking to the shul I thought about that moving *midrash* that explains how Moshe went looking for the lost lamb. Moshe Rabbeinu was tending his flock when he noticed a lamb running away. He followed it until it finally stopped at a clear pool of water and drank. Moshe gathered up the lamb and carried it back to the flock, saying, "If I had known you were thirsty, I would have carried you to the water." Surely this was similar to what the Avtzons were doing here in Hong Kong, tenderly gathering the lost sheep of Israel.

When we arrived at the shul in the Coda Plaza, Mid-level, the men had already finished davening and we were directed to the social hall, where we would be eating the Shabbos meal.

The Avtzons had a very eclectic community, but everyone was very friendly, coming over to introduce themselves and wish us a good Shabbos.

During the meal the conversation was lively and diverse. The meal had been catered by one of the members of the community. I was so impressed with the food I couldn't help but wonder if she would one day write a cookbook.

The men sang *zemiros* and we continued to talk and enjoy the lovely atmosphere. When we concluded the meal, Rabbi Avtzon gave a brief *d'var Torah* on *Parashas Va'eschanan*. He focused on the haftarah and spoke eloquently on how it was one of the seven of consolation. He mentioned briefly the *matzav*, the situation in Israel, and used the words of the prophet Yeshayah to comfort our hearts, "*Nachamu, Nachamu* — Comfort, comfort My people."

After Rabbi Avtzon finished his *d'var Torah*, he introduced me with the following words: "I received an e-mail from a woman named Ahuvah Gray, saying that she was going to Australia and South Africa to lecture and she would be stopping in Hong Kong. However, since I had never heard of Ahuvah Gray or her book, *My Sister, the Jew*, I hesitated to invite her to our community. I needed to find out who Ahuvah was. Two weeks later, my dear friend from Melbourne, Australia, Samuel Roden, phoned me and told me that he was arranging Ms. Gray's lecture tour. I said, 'Samuel, could you tell me something about Ahuvah Gray?' He answered me, 'Mordechai, she is the modern day Ruth!' So now I have the privilege to present to you 'the modern day Ruth.' "

I rose up to speak, trembling slightly. After all, I thought, who could be deserving of such a title? Regaining my composure I started to speak and to share my story. Yes, Jews are responsible for the whole world and responsible for each other as well. Somehow the fact that we are one *neshamah* was in my heart that night. I shared with my audience how Rebbetzin Henkin, the founder of Nishmat, a center for women's higher Torah study in Bayit Vegan, gave a *seudah* in honor of my conversion and closed the entire center for the occasion. Here I was, a woman from another country, another religion, another world, and when I joined the Jewish people after my long road, a whole school full of young religious women joined me to celebrate. The people in that room all came from different places and different backgrounds, but the same principle held: one *neshamah*, one heartbeat, in a shul in Hong Kong.

At the conclusion of the lecture, the questions began.

"Ahuvah, could you tell us what it is like being an African American Jewess living in Israel?"

I said, "May I rephrase the question? If you are asking, 'Have I ever experienced any racial biases,' the answer is no. The reason being that I moved from one Black neighborhood to another Black neighborhood. I feel comfortable in Bayit Vegan because all the men walk around in black suits and hats!"

As usual, the room filled with laughter. The atmosphere was warm and friendly, but the next question was tougher.

"Ahuvah, I have heard horrible stories about the *beis din*, the Jewish court of law, in Jerusalem. Can you share with us what that experience was like?"

"I discussed this subject at length in my book, *My Sister, the Jew*, in a chapter entitled 'Harvard Conversion.' I worked in corporate America for thirty-plus years and signed two- and three-million-dollar contracts, in addition to owning my business.

With all the difficulties that this kind of career presented — my conversion, which took two years, was far more challenging.

"But before you start condemning the system, please try to understand the why of it. The rabbis have every right to turn an individual away. When a non-Jew comes before them proclaiming he wants to be a Jew, they are required to make it difficult. In fact, the halachah is alluded to in the book of Ruth. Naomi entreats Ruth, the first female convert, to go back to her people. But Ruth courageously responds, 'Your people are my people, and your God is my God; where you die, I will die, and there I will be buried.'

"On another level, what I have discovered is that the real challenge isn't the conversion process, it's how I live my daily life after having taken upon myself the 613 mitzvos. The reason the rabbis make it so difficult is to test our sincerity, and if the person is genuine then they will eventually succeed.

"We also know that when Mashiach comes there will be no more conversions. So all of the souls that are meant to convert have to return during these days to rejoin our people."

Rabbi Avtzon himself posed the last question. "Ahuvah, could you please tell the audience why you chose Orthodox Judaism?"

"That's an excellent question. In my previous life we used to sing a song entitled 'Climbing Jacob's Ladder.' There's a verse in that song that says, 'Every rung goes higher and higher.' I wanted to practice the highest level of observance within Judaism. I personally feel that Orthodox Judaism is a very high standard. I don't feel like I have reached the top of the ladder at the moment, but I am still climbing. The people in my neighborhood are excellent role models. I am so grateful to Hashem for placing me in such a holy environment. It was quite a leap from my old neighborhood. I may have gone from black to black, but I also went from *chol* to *kodesh*."

After my talk, I could relax and enjoy the rest of Shabbos in Hong Kong. I savored the good food, the warm and friendly atmosphere, and the words of Torah. I remembered how the Shinto priest spoke of the combination of material and spiritual development, and I knew that I was living what he was only describing.

At the third meal, *seudah shelishis*, men and women ate separately. I gave a brief second talk to the women on the parashah and spoke a bit more about the returning of a lost object. I touched on Shira Taylor's story, where the lost object was a Jewish *neshamah*. I pointed out that the story of a young Orthodox Jew returning to her people has special meaning to me, as a convert — I, too, have returned to my people. Just as it states in the Midrash, Hashem offered the Torah to each of the nations before offering it to the people of Israel. While the majority of each nation rejected the Torah, there was a minority that was prepared to accept it. The *ger tzedek* Avraham ben Avraham, a Polish prince who converted during the time of the Vilna Gaon, commented on this *midrash*. He suggests that each convert possesses the soul of one of those among the nations of the world who was prepared to accept the Torah before it was offered to the people of Israel at Mount Sinai. (According to another tradition, it was the Vilna Gaon who said this insight.)

I ended my story by quoting from Shira's letter. "There is a concept in Judaism whereby the merit of observing mitzvos and doing good deeds goes both to the doer and to the person who inspired those actions. At 120 Ahuvah will have lived a relatively short time as a Jew, having converted at age fifty-one. But she will also have lived many lifetimes as a Torah-observant Jew, as the merit of the mitzvos of the people she has inspired mounts. Ahuvah can consider the years of Torah growth ahead of me as her own."

Our Sages tell us that every person is an entire world, and that each Jew is responsible fore each other. "*Kol Yisrael areivim zeh bazeh.*" Hashem had made me the messenger that brought about Shira Taylor's spiritual reawakening, and in doing so we both created a fundamental shift in the world. Her world changed dramatically. My world expanded and was enriched, her story continues to inspire other people, and the chain of responsibility goes on.

The rest of my trip went by too quickly. One breathless shopping spree, in which one of the members of the Jewish community bargained with the street merchants in Chinese for me, a gracious and emotional good-bye to the Avtzons, who had become my friends in so short a time, and then it was off to the airport once again.

As we started to ascend, I saw once again the beautiful turquoise blue water and all the little clusters of islands that surround Japan. Each island was an entity in and of itself, separate and distinct from its neighbor. Each has its own culture and is responsible to its own nation. To paraphrase what the Shinto priest said to Rabbi Zeller, "Wonderful people, wonderful culture, but not responsible for the whole world." The Jewish people was chosen to be different. Our consciousness, our impact, our obligations encompass a partnership with the Almighty.

From the sheep that Moshe Rabbeinu held in his arms, to the Jewish community that Rabbi Avtzon established in Hong Kong, to the Jewish home that Shira Taylor will one day build: "Jews responsible for the whole world!"

Chapter Five

The Jewish Connection: Down Under in Space, Backwards and Forwards in Time

*T*wenty years ago, in a different lifetime, a friend and I approached a beautiful building in Sydney, Australia. I was traveling throughout the continent on a familiarization trip sponsored by the airline I worked for. The building was not on my itinerary, but I felt drawn to it and went to take a closer look.

I don't know how, but suddenly I recognized the building for what it was — a synagogue. I felt this sudden, inexplicable yearning in my heart to go inside. In all my travels throughout the world, I had never experienced a feeling like this before. What was happening to me?

People in the Northern Hemisphere always have a vision of Australians walking upside down in their bottom half of the world. Surprise! All the Australians I met "down under" were walking right side up. What was turned upside down that day, to my mind, were my own feelings as I approached the beautiful building in Sydney. I had never even been in a synagogue before. Why, then, did I feel such a longing to go into this building, which I discovered to be the Great Synagogue of Sydney? What was attracting my mind, my heart, my soul to this place that I knew so little of but that felt like home, nonetheless?

It was a haunting question, one that I couldn't answer at the time. My friend wasn't religiously inclined, and I did not want to embarrass her. Silently, I ignored the voice within me that told me to go into the building and continued my touring.

On that first trip to Australia, I viewed the country through the spectacles of a tourist. I enjoyed the tropical weather and beautiful palm trees of Carnes. I admired the sunset over the Pacific Ocean, a magnificent show of orange and yellow and fiery purple. What impressed me most on this whirlwind trip, though, was the Great Barrier Reef that is located off the northeast coast of Australia, where scuba divers come from all over the world to see the wonders down under the sea.

I was enthralled by the stories of Australian history. I learned about the indigenous Aboriginal people, wondering if there could be some ancestral connection. From their features I didn't think so. Their appearance was more Asian than African.

I hugged a koala bear, admired Sydney Harbor and Opera House, and walked along the tranquil boardwalk of the Gold Coast, humming softly under my breath. As I toured the land, smiling at the inevitable greeting of "Good day, mate," I looked like every other American tourist enjoying the relaxed atmosphere of this interesting country.

I took lots of things back from that trip — a stuffed koala bear, pictures, good memories — and I could not leave without visiting a jewelry shop and purchasing an opal ring and bracelet. But I also took back a sense of an opportunity missed, a hole left unfilled, a moment of destiny that I had not yet faced. My trip felt unfinished.

Unfinished, that is, until two decades later, when I began finishing it, not in Australia, but in a room in Yerushalayim.

For twenty years later, the Holy One, blessed be He, sent me to Nishmat, a center for women's higher Torah study in Bayit Vegan. There I met a teacher named Rebbetzin Riva Sperling. She turned out to be the daughter of Rabbi Appel, the rabbi of that same shul that spoke to my heart that day, so long ago and so far away in Sydney, Australia!

Rebbetzin Riva taught a class about *tzenius*, modesty. I had stopped wearing pants and slitted skirts years before, but her class deepened my understanding of the concept. "The glory of the King's daughter is within" (*Tehillim* 45:14). When I realized my teacher's connection to the synagogue in Sydney, it occurred to me that my learning from the rabbi's daughter before entering the synagogue was meant to be — was indeed *hashgachah peratis*, Divine providence. In order to become a *frum* woman, I had to understand that the synagogue was the public domain of the community; my own place to develop and to grow was within, within the confines of my classroom, within the confines of Jewish homes.

My original feeling about the synagogue — a place that was

new, yet that I recognized, somehow — was akin to my feelings about Nishmat itself. During my first few months there I would call my sister weekly and explain what I had absorbed about my new lifestyle with great enthusiasm.

"Nellie, I have never seen anything like this. It's all so new — and yet all so familiar! My teachers are so committed and extremely knowledgeable. They come from religious homes like us. Remember how we used to think Mother and Dad were too strict? You won't believe it, but I don't think so now. Ironically, they were teaching us Jewish values."

Life sometimes seems to me to be shaped like circles on circles on circles. The circle of my experience in Australia began long ago, with a wistful feeling of longing for a building. That particular circle closed when I made the connection between the building and a teacher at Nishmat.

But another circle opened at Nishmat. It started when my first book, *My Sister, the Jew*, was published. To express my appreciation in some small way to Rebbetzin Henkin, founder of Nishmat, I autographed a copy of my book to present to the school as a gift.

When I went to the office, the *rebbetzin* was in a meeting. I had many books to deliver, so I decided to leave it with her secretary. Before I left, though, I went to the half-open door where the *rebbetzin* was conducting the meeting and held my book up, gesturing toward the secretary's office to indicate that I would leave a book with her.

Instantly I saw a huge smile and I heard a big "*mazal tov!*" The *rebbetzin* excused herself and ran to the door to embrace me with one of her customized motherly hugs. I was escorted into

her office and introduced to the two women in the room. She
told the women that my book was out and said, "We have to
make a *l'chaim*."

By then the entire staff had joined in the celebration. The
secretary, Michal Stone, went and got the grape juice and
glasses. The *rebbetzin* made a speech expressing how proud she
was of me and that Nishmat was happy to have had me as a student for one year.

Before I left, Michal inquired if my lecture tours would take
me to Australia. I told her that I had plans to lecture only in
America.

"If you ever decide you want to go to Australia, my parents
will help you." And from that opening of a circle, I found myself
a year later flying out to Australia once again, with Michal's
mother, Frances Stone, one of a team of ten faithful organizers
from down under!

As the plane in Hong Kong took off to Australia, I thought
about one of my memorable Shabbosos with the
Feldmans. In fact, they were all memorable. When I first
started going I went because Rebbetzin Feldman's *cholent* was
so delicious. After I matured a bit I went for the *divrei Torah* and
the *cholent*.

Rebbetzin Leah Feldman always had a unique way of making every guest feel special. When she introduced me, she said,
"This is Ahuvah Gray, former flight attendant and minister.
Now she is a messenger for Hashem and flying higher and
higher."

Flying higher — I had been to Australia once, working for an
airline, but now I was returning, a *frum* Jewess who could not

only enter a synagogue but who was at home in any religious Jewish house of prayer. Flying higher and higher, indeed!

Through the spectacles of a Jewess, I reviewed the historical information that I had collected on Australia. The first Jewish services in Victoria were held in a private home in Melbourne in 1840, with fifty-seven Jews present. The East Melbourne Hebrew Congregation was founded in 1857. All the early synagogues in Australia were known as Anglo-Orthodox, following the British United Synagogue, and highly acculturated and patriotic to their host country. After World War I, both Reform and Orthodox synagogues could be found.

Between the two world wars there was an influx of new immigrants, bringing with them activists from the Zionist movement, Yiddish cultural activities, and left-wing Jewish groups.

Australian Jewry became even more diverse with the arrival of ten thousand German and Austrian Jewish refugees in 1933 to 1940, and about twenty-five thousand Holocaust survivors, mostly from Poland and Hungary, in 1946 to 1957.

What I learned about Australian Jewry from books was interesting, but it didn't prepare me for what I learned about Australian Jews from my short visit with them. They have hearts as vast as the outback, the immense desert that makes up so much of Australia, and they make their guests feel as cozy and welcome as a kangaroo baby (called a joey) must feel when it is snuggled up in its mother's pouch.

In Melbourne, I stayed at the home of the Herzog family. Mary Herzog asked me what I liked to eat. I told her that for breakfast I liked cranberry juice and bananas with coffee. "That's all?" she replied. When her husband, Izzy, came home a little later, in he walked with twelve bottles of cranberry juice and three pounds of bananas. Australian hospitality!

Our dinner was delightful. We talked a lot about the lecture tour and what I would like to do during my spare time — not that my busy schedule gave me much time for touring. Mary prepared the best lamb chops and rice I have ever had. We had a lovely salad and fresh bread that Izzy had bought at the bakery that morning as well as wonderful pastries for dessert. I could easily see that the only thing that was going to be problematic was maintaining my weight. The next morning we had more pastry and fresh bread from the bakery, and Mary was complaining because she said I didn't eat enough.

Frances Stone was constantly in contact with me, as were Eve and Michael Gordon and Les Brown. They kept me informed about all the forthcoming lectures. Frances let me know she was available if I needed anything. Her parting words every day were, "Ahuvah, I am here to serve you and make your visit pleasant. If you need anything, please don't hesitate to call." Between her help and the Herzogs' hospitality, I felt pampered indeed!

But I hadn't come to Australia simply to enjoy myself — there was work to be done! I began a strenuous round of lectures all over the country. In Melbourne I spoke for numerous schools and women's organizations. The list is too extensive to include totally. The schools included Ohel Channah Ladies' Seminary — Chabad, King David School, Mount Scopus, Bialik, and Neshei Chabad. I was scheduled to close my first Shabbos in Melbourne with a *melaveh malkah* for ladies and girls from Adass Israel at the home of Mrs. Aggie Brody. Afterwards I would be flying higher and higher to Brisbane, lecturing for

Rabbi Levi Jaffe, and then off to the Gold Coast, lecturing for Rabbi Nir Gurevitch, before returning to home base at the Herzogs'.

Before I realized it I was seated on the platform facing an audience of 350 in my first lecture, which had been organized by Kehilat Tiferet Yisroel.

The kind words of Rabbi Meir Rabi, the congregation's rabbi, reverberated in the auditorium of Werdiger Hall. "Our Sages say we have many opportunities to learn from many teachers. They conclude that it is from our students that we learn the most. Rabbi Yehoshua elaborated on that and stated that we can learn the most from a child. He related the following story:

"Rabbi Yehoshua was traveling in an unfamiliar area when he came to a fork in the road. He saw a child sitting nearby and asked him which was the best way to the city.

" 'This path doesn't lead directly to the city; it's long but it's short. The other path leads directly to the city; it is short, but it is long,' was the reply.

"It seemed to the rabbi that the child was teasing, but he didn't want to challenge the child, so he decided to take the short path. Although the road led directly to his destination, he encountered many obstacles and finally retraced his steps. He found the child again and challenged him.

" 'Didn't you say this was the shortest path?'

"And the child responded, 'Did I not also tell you that it was the longer path?' "

Rabbi Rabi closed by saying, "How many of us when we ran into obstacles in life chose the shorter path? But Ahuvah has chosen the longer path. She has taken a path that eventually reaches the destination."

I was very touched by his remarks. The emcee followed by saying that she too was a convert, and she stated, "We are all on a journey. It's been a while since Sinai, but Ahuvah is here to share with us tonight her soul's journey."

As I walked to the microphone the thought of retracing my footsteps and taking that longer path lingered in my mind. It had, indeed, been a long path that had brought me back to Australia, but this time it was a full circle. That day when I wanted to go into a synagogue but had no idea why seemed so far away. On the other hand, the days I spent as a child with my mother and grandmother didn't seem that far away at all. In fact, I focused my lecture on the hospitality that my mother displayed to homeless people when we were children and on the acts of kindness of my grandmother, connecting my memories to the wonderful hospitality I had received at the home of the Herzogs — perhaps it was actually in the *zechus* of my mother and grandmother!

I ended the lecture by telling the story of Shira Taylor. Once again, I asked if there were any South Africans in the audience who could read the e-mail. To my surprise, almost half the audience raised their hands!

Immediately afterward we started the question-and-answer session.

"Ahuvah, do you think your mother and grandmother would be proud of you?"

"I think so. The seeds of my spiritual life were planted at their table. I think they would be proud to see how I have grown in their spirit!"

The next question came from a girl sitting way in the back.

"Ahuvah, what is living in Jerusalem like for you? Was the transition an easy one?"

"At my age it wasn't an easy transition, but I have great support from my community. The families in Bayit Vegan have been instrumental in helping me refine the true meaning of love. I think I am just beginning to understand what it means to be one *neshamah*."

"Ahuvah, do you look forward to getting married in the near future?"

"Yes, do you know anybody?"

Everyone started laughing and so did I. And with that laughter, and Mary's hugs, the lecture came to a close.

Chapter Six

Flying Higher and Higher

*T*he next weeks were busy — I was wined and dined by the Herzogs, whose hospitality gave me the strength to deliver some twenty-five lectures all over Australia. I met hundreds of people, but a number of incidents stand out. There was the lecture I gave in the Yavneh School in Melbourne, which had a newly appointed principal, Rabbi Chanina Rabinowitz. After my talk, two students asked very profound questions. I love lecturing to young people because they are very honest and don't have the apprehension that we adults have.

The first question, "Ahuvah, do you think you are as Jewish as I am?" left me feeling very humbled.

I answered in a very slow, calm voice. "I have been asked numerous questions as I have traveled around the world, but I think you just touched my heart. Yes, I do feel I am as Jewish as you are. In fact, I had lots of birthing pains to remind me that I am a Jew. You were born a Jew and I took the long road home."

The second question was less complicated. "Ahuvah, you

worked so hard to become a Jew and we don't have to do anything. Do you think it's fair?"

"Because I had to toil for the Torah I feel that it was all worthwhile — and there are very few things in life that are fair."

The next morning I had a book signing at Gold's bookstore. I was grateful to hear from people who came for an autographed copy of my book that their friends and relatives who had heard me at Mrs. Brody's house, the Adass women, had enjoyed the lecture. I wasn't accustomed to such a reserved audience. However, I was assured that they had enjoyed the lecture immensely.

Following the book signing, Eve Gordon and I were off to Mount Scopus, a high school with a lovely coeducation campus. Frances had already explained to me that in Melbourne they don't have the problem of assimilation and intermarriage because all the Jewish children get a Jewish education. Her words were like music to my ears.

When we arrived we were surrounded by youths. During the lecture, I noticed two girls who looked familiar in the audience. Once again I closed out with Shira's story.

At the conclusion of the lecture the two girls came over to me and said, "Ahuvah, do you remember us?"

"Yes, but where did we meet?" I replied anxiously.

"We attended the Aish HaTorah Fellowships Program with Shira," one explained. "Thank you for sharing her story with us. Your story touched all our lives that day. I am davening with much more *kavanah* now."

The other chimed in, "I am reading *Tehillim* every day because of the story you shared about your grandmother. It's an odyssey, Ahuvah."

Before we parted, I embraced both girls and thanked them for sharing their personal stories with me.

My Shabbosos in Australia were especially interesting. I had always wanted to bake challah, but I had found myself too busy in Israel to try it. *Erev Shabbos*, after davening, Mary informed me that her daughter, Ilana, had challah baking classes in her home, so I found myself baking challah for the very first time in Melbourne, Australia! Not only did I get to learn braiding techniques, but I was also able to share with Ilana what Rebbetzin Heyman had told me about challah baking.

"Baking challos is a *tikun* for the sin of Chavah, and it is also used as a *zechus* to have children. Because the actions of Chavah brought death into the world, the act of baking challos could bring life." Braiding, baking, and talking Torah, down under.... Flying higher and higher....

I was invited out for all the meals that first Shabbos. On Friday, before leaving Mary's, I explained to Frances that my rabbi's *minhag* is not to carry on Shabbos. Even though the *eiruv* was reliable, I wanted to follow my *rav's minhag*. So Frances graciously agreed to carry my glasses to the home of Shoshie and Shelomo Koppel of Congregation Adass Israel.

After the meal, Mary's cousin's husband walked me back to the Herzogs'. He offered to carry my glasses home. As we were leaving my host family, he looked at his wife and said, "You know, I have always wanted to be a *Shabbos goy*." Laughter reverberated throughout the room.

My first Shabbos morning in Australia as a Jewess. I was excited because after all those years of thinking about going to a synagogue in Australia, the time had actually come. Even though it was a long journey, inherently it was a soul journey worth waiting for.

As Frances and I walked to Rabbi Rabi's shul, Kehilat Tiferet Yisroel, my anticipation of the day's events increased. The services seemed very fast to me; I suppose I had become more accustomed to the slower pace of my shul in Bayit Vegan, HaGra. During my short talk to the congregants, I remarked gently that davening was a bit fast for me. Rabbi Rabi came over at the end of the lecture and thanked me for pointing this out.

We went to the Rabbi Rabi's home for lunch. It was a short walk from shul. Upon our arrival Rebbetzin Rabi gave me a nice hearty welcome and introduced their seven children. Then we sat down to a lovely Shabbos meal.

After the meal Rabbi Rabi's parents came over and Mr. Moshe Rabi told us how he had first arrived in Australia. He was a survivor of a ship called the *Dunera*, a British boat that took displaced German Jews from England to Australia. With his voice trembling, Mr. Rabi said that as they were traveling they heard gunshots. "We later found out that it was torpedoes passing underneath the boat."

They had to start throwing books and other objects overboard to lighten the ship's load. As Divine providence would have it, the commander of the German vessel spotted the books, which were mostly in German, and assumed that they were German prisoners of war. Thus, he allowed the ship to travel safely for the rest of its journey. The ship went on to Australia, where its passengers were interned under difficult conditions for the duration of World War II. Mr. Rabi spoke quietly but with deep emotion. His words were so touching I was almost moved to tears.

Divine providence was the theme of many of the stories that I heard in Australia. Rabbi Nojowitz, a *talmid* of my *abba*, shared with me a wonderful story. He and nine other rabbis were sent to Australia in 1981 by Rabbi Shneur Kotler, *zt"l*, to start the *kollel* there.

"One time the *kollel* men had to be paid and we were short seven thousand dollars. I called one of the supporters of the *kollel*, hoping that he would be willing to cover that amount. Before I even had the chance to tell him the reason for my call, the phone line went dead. A moment later there was a knock at the front door. When I opened it, I saw someone from Federal Express standing there with a letter. Inside it was a check from Hong Kong made out for seven thousand dollars."

My circle of friends had definitely expanded over my four-and-a-half-week lecture tour in Melbourne. I couldn't believe that my visit had gone by so quickly. On Sunday I would be flying off to Brisbane, then to Sydney, and from there to the Gold Coast and back to Melbourne for the concluding lecture.

When Mary and I had breakfast as usual on *erev shabbos*, she told me that she and Izzy would be visiting the Gold Coast at the same time that I would be lecturing. How wonderful it would be to see them a few days before I would be leaving Australia.

I spent my last Shabbos in Melbourne with Vicki Gordon, Mary Herzog's daughter and her family, and Shabbos lunch with Laibl and Leah Wolf, the daughter and son-in-law of my neighbor Mrs. Kesel. Laibl is the author of *Practical Kabbalah* (New York: Random House, 1999).

On Sunday morning I was busy packing because Eve was coming to take me to the airport. When she arrived, we took my luggage down the stairs, and then I went in the kitchen to thank Mary and give her a hug. I started crying because being there with her and Izzy was like having parents again. In her usual cheerful way, Mary said, "Ahuvah, we thoroughly enjoyed you as well, and we will be seeing you next week on the Gold Coast. Please stop crying."

When I arrived at the airport in Brisbane, Rabbi Jaffe picked me up. It was lovely to see the sunshine because it had been cloudy and overcast in Melbourne. We went directly to Rabbi Jaffe's home. When we arrived Rebbetzin Jaffe served lunch, after which I went to my room to relax before the lecture that evening.

It was lovely to visit Brisbane again. I had been there once before on my first trip to Australia. Rabbi Jaffe and I drove to a synagogue in the center of town where the lecture was to be held. We had a very nice-sized crowd. During the question-and-answer session after the lecture, I mentioned that I would be going to South Africa after Australia. Once again I discovered that there were many South Africans in the audience. At the end of the lecture about ten South Africans came to me and assured me that I would really enjoy my visit to South Africa. As they spoke, I knew my circle of friends was broadening.

The next day I was on a plane again to Sydney, where I was the guest of Judy Levitan and her husband, Tommy Sterling. Judy and I had studied together at Nishmat. What a team in

Sydney — it reminded me a bit of New York. Judy and her husband were both lawyers, and on *erev Shabbos* they both arrived home just in time to put the food on the *blech* and get everything ready for Shabbos. I offered to help, but they had such a routine they didn't need it.

We had a lovely quiet Friday night meal at home alone. My main lecture was at Jewish Learning Center, headed by Rabbi Dovid Blackman, after lunch, and then I had one more lecture on Sunday.

On Monday morning, I woke up early and found myself packing for another trip to the airport. On the way I asked the driver to drive by the Great Synagogue. I couldn't leave Sydney without closing that circle.

Once I boarded the airplane I fastened my seat belt and enjoyed the scenic view as I traveled to the Gold Coast Coolangatta Airport.

Upon my arrival, Rebbetzin Gurevitch picked me up at the airport. When we arrived at their home she introduced me to Rabbi Gurevitch. My lecture in Gold Coast was scheduled for that evening. I would be seeing Izzy and Mary the next day and then leaving the following morning.

We had a large crowd at the lecture. The Gold Coast is mostly a retirement community. The question-and-answer session was lengthy and to my disappointment I ran out of books, an author's nightmare.

The next morning I flew from the Gold Coast back to Melbourne for the closing lecture at Blake Street Hebrew Congregation.

Rabbi Yirmi Garfunkel, another *talmid* of Rabbi Heyman,

introduced me. I appreciated his sense of humor and lively spirit as he spoke. "The first story I heard about Ahuvah Gray was that she does not carry on Shabbos. The second story was that she doesn't leave Eretz Yisrael without a *berachah* from Rav Elyashiv. This is the conclusion of her lecture series in Melbourne, and she is here to share with us her humble beginning and lofty conclusions."

With his introduction echoing in my mind, I began to speak, hoping that my lecture would express the loving kindness I had been shown during the entirety of my visit to Melbourne.

Rabbi Garfunkel closed the lecture with the following comments:

"I've heard Ahuvah lecture three times over the course of her visit with us, and I believe this was the best of her lecture series in Melbourne. The title of the lecture tonight was 'Humble Beginnings and Lofty Conclusions.' Surely Ahuvah has inspired us and broadened our circle by sharing her soul's journey with us. My prayer is that we all have benefit from her journey."

Hashgachah peratis. Divine providence. Why was it meant for me to come back to Australia after so many years, to meet such fine people, to enjoy such *hachnasas orchim*? Perhaps the stories I told touched some hearts in a way that I may never know. Perhaps I learned something from the wonderful people that I met, something that will guide me as I continue to learn to fly higher and higher. The ways of Hashem are not always clear to us.

But there was one change that my trip definitely did effect, and for me it is a clear instance of Hashem's *hashgachah peratis.* I began my trip with the memory of my first desire to enter a synagogue, a desire that wasn't fulfilled at the time. Twenty years later, on my last Shabbos in Melbourne, another circle was closed. I went to daven once again at Rabbi Rabi's shul, and one of my new Australian friends from the congregation came over to me and said, "Ahuvah, did you notice that we're all davening more slowly now?"

Twenty years later, after my long, long road, I had made a difference in a synagogue down under!

Chapter Seven

A Soul Resonance

The next thing I knew, I was getting ready to fly higher and higher — on to South Africa!

But before I was airborne, I had one more hurdle on the ground down under — twenty-four kilos too much luggage.

A new friend from Australia, Eve Gordon, took me to the airport and was with me when the ticketing agent informed me that my luggage was overweight. It was the first time I encountered this problem, and I tried not to feel dismayed.

"What are you carrying that's so heavy?" the agent asked.

"Books," I replied, adding with a warm smile, "I am here on a lecture tour from Israel."

"Well, let me see if I can go in the back and find you a box so we can take some of the books out of the luggage and make them easier to carry."

Eve stood there, looking shocked. When the ticket agent came back she helped me unpack the books that were in my luggage, and we put them in the box together. Then the ticket agent sealed the box with tape. She allowed me to check all three pieces without any extra charge. I thanked her profusely and my friend watched in utter disbelief.

When we left the ticket counter and I headed for the gate, Eve said, "Ahuvah, I've never seen anything like that in all my years of traveling, especially out of Melbourne Airport."

"Eve, it happens to me all the time, I assume because of the *berachah* from Rabbi Elyashiv."

"You mean this isn't the first time this happened?"

"No, things like this happen all the time. I think it's called *chein*."

Eve and I laughed and embraced, and so with smiles and *berachos* and an extra box of books, I found myself heading towards South Africa.

As the plane soared through layers of clouds, my thoughts flew ahead to my reunion with Shira Taylor. Eighteen months had passed since that chilly morning in December 2000, when Shira, a twenty-one-year-old student from Johannesburg, South Africa, walked into my life. Though we had only met once since then, we had grown close in our letters as we explored difficult questions and issues together. With her courage to think the unthinkable and ask the unanswerable, she had given me honest glimpses into her life. Moreover, her generous consent to my sharing her letters with my audiences has had a tremendous impact upon the lives of Jews around the world.

As I sat on the plane, I reviewed in my mind some of the questions we had faced together. I remember vividly her second letter to me:

Dear Ahuvah,

My issue at the moment is how to love Hashem and trust Him without secretly having a prescription of how I think things should be and expecting things to go my way. I am scared that if I tell Hashem I accept everything He does, then that will give Him "permission" to bring tragedy into my life. It's so hard to feel totally safe with Hashem because I don't know what He'll do next, and whatever He does, I'll have to accept it. It's so hard to trust Him; to trust that whatever happens is good, because it's from His love and compassion. Thanks for the last e-mail about emunah. Wise words from a wise woman. What a level!! I am so far away, but I am learning at a seminary and am asking Hashem every day to help me have emunah in Him and to not expect things to be how I want them to be.

Ahuvah, do you think Hashem knows what pain is? Emotional pain, like despair, or the feelings of abandonment or loss, or fear or anger? Do you think He knows what physical pain is? For example, does He know how it feels to stub your toe, or to be a burn victim, chas veshalom?

My question is, does Hashem know what it is to be a neshamah, to be a human being? Does He know what it's like? It's a stupid question, I know, but it bothers me. Because He can't expect so much of us if He doesn't know how hard life is. It was so easy for Him to create the world; nothing is hard for Him Does He know what it's like for us?

Have a good Shabbos. Thank you for all your enthusiasm and emunah that reaches across the ocean between us and gives me chizuk.

One of the things that I answered Shira was that Hashem knows us because He created within us the *tzelem Elokim*. We were created in His image and likeness. I continued,

My dear Shira, you're not far away. It's just an illusion, just what the yetzar hara wants you to think. In reality, you are so close. What I have learned in life is that I don't trust the majority of the thoughts that run through my mind. But what I can trust is Hashem's word.

I also tried to show Shira how her words, her questions, were giving a message of searching and of hope to all who heard them. In this time of fear, the *chizuk* she gave us was especially critical.

And now here I was, about to land in South Africa. I was so looking forward to seeing Shira in person again, to ask our questions and search for answers face to face.

My mind shifted from Shira's letter to another letter, one written by an anonymous donor who was the sponsor of this segment of my lecture tour. He had purchased my book, *My Sister, the Jew,* after reading an article about it in the *Jewish Press*. When he finished reading the book, he wrote me the following words:

Dear Ms. Gray,

Thank you very much for your inspirational book. I enjoyed reading your story very much; it really touches the neshamah. I read it during Sukkos and was really inspired by it. I told my wife she would enjoy reading it as well, even though she is FFB — religious from birth. I'm hoping to buy the book for some others whom I believe could benefit from it. Actually, everyone could benefit from it. Obviously you've developed a very special relationship with Hashem. May it continue to blossom.

This morning I read in an article that the Chafetz Chaim, zt"l, once said, "At first, I intended to change the whole world but soon real- ized it wasn't possible. Then I sought to change my entire city, but that too was beyond my reach. Finally I tried my entire family, but even that was not feasible. I then decided to try to change just one person — my-

self." Rav Wasserman, his beloved student, added, "Through himself he changed the entire world." I will be bold enough to say that this also applies to you.

As I peered through the window once more before landing, I wondered how I would feel in Africa, the land where my ancestors once lived, the land from which they entered slavery.

I entered the airport and took my first steps on the South African turf. Peering through the crowds, I remembered Alex Haley's best-selling book, *Roots.* When he had successfully completed years or researching his ancestral tribe, he joyfully proclaimed to the world, "I found you, you old African you." A bit to my surprise, I found that I was less interested in looking for "old Africans" than I was in looking for religious Jews, especially the family that was coming to meet me. My desire was to find a religious Jew, so I could feel safe — and more at home.

After leaving the baggage claim, I was met by Rebbetzin Leiba Moffson, whose husband had arranged my lecture tour, and two of her daughters. I greeted them warmly, feeling very relieved. Rebbetzin Moffson's husband, Shmuel, works for Ohr Somayach Joahannesburg, which is headed by Rabbi Yechezkel Auerbach.

We proceeded to the car. As we drove, I got an almost unreal feeling that something that was familiar was also unfamiliar. Suddenly I realized that it was because all the cars seemed to be driving on the wrong side of the road. Rebbetzin Moffson explained that South Africa followed the British way of driving on the left side of the road. But that didn't explain the car that I noticed that kept pulling up close to us and at one point at a stoplight started backing up, instead of going forward. Remembering all the horrible stories I had heard about carjackings and drive-by shootings in South Africa, I shifted in my seat uneasily. The *rebbetzin* noticed and said gently, "Don't pay any attention to the driver next to us, Ahuvah. I am sure he will sort things out momentarily. Just a new driver who has his gears all wrong!" We all laughed and her comments released the tension that had been building up inside me.

To lighten the atmosphere, Rebbetzin Moffson began to fill me in on the details of my lectures. I was confident that Rabbi Moffson had meticulously taken care of everything relevant to my visit. "Ahuvah, our community is so excited that you are here," one of the Moffson girls said enthusiastically. "You'll be speaking at my school tomorrow."

Despite the *rebbetzin*'s assurances, I couldn't help but notice the security arrangements wherever we went. At the entrance to the housing complex, a guard waved us on. The *rebbetzin* told me I would be staying at the Zulbergs' home instead of the Taylors' because the Taylors had gotten unexpected guests.

When I entered the house a familiar face greeted me. "I am Ruthie, and you know me from Bayit Vegan." It was lovely to have an acquaintance from home welcome me into her parents' home. Mrs. Linda Zulberg, Ruthie's mother, introduced herself and took me immediately to my room. She said that Shira had already called and would be picking me up in two hours to have dinner with her family. One of the servants graciously took my heavy luggage to my room on the second floor, where I found all the luxuries of a five-star hotel at my disposal. Fresh flowers, slippers at the foot of the bed, a fruit basket of nuts and raisins, and an assortment of herbal teas and coffee. I turned the percolator on as I started to unpack.

I had just enough time to relax a bit and enjoy the accommodations before Shira arrived promptly at 7:30 p.m. Linda brought her to my room. What a reunion! We were both so excited we began talking at the same time. Half laughing, half crying, we caught up quickly, sharing the highlights of the many months we hadn't seen each other.

We continued to talk as we drove to her home. Shira explained that people pause at a stop sign and keep going for safety reasons. The sight of some of those hostile faces made even me, an African American, feel a bit frightened and uncomfortable. I recalled my first visit to Harlem, in New York City. In Chicago, my neighborhood was respectable and safe. After having read and heard about Harlem and sections like it, I decided to visit there. Seeing a ghetto with gang members hanging around on street corners was a frightening experience. My visit was brief and ended by my telling the taxi driver, "Thank you very much, you can take me back to Park Plaza Hotel, please!"

When we arrived at Shira's home I met her sister, brother-in-law, and their child who were visiting. Her parents came to welcome me. After all the introductions we sat down to a beautifully adorned table with a delicious variety of food. It was a Shabbos meal served during the week. My only regret was that I couldn't eat more. I should have fasted for a week to prepare myself for the South African hospitality!

The conversation at the table was as rich and nourishing as the food — soul food, indeed! I began by telling the Taylors, "Your daughter's story is famous!" I described how seminary girls in Israel, America, Australia, Belgium, and England had listened, mesmerized, to Shira's story. Some had told me privately that they had the same thoughts, but were too afraid to express them verbally.

Shira's family listened eagerly to every word as I continued, "Surely the reason that Shira expresses herself so openly and candidly is because of your loving tolerance and patience. The thing that touches people the most is her honesty. Obviously you are the source of her strength and as a result of observing your lives she learned the valuable lesson of integrity. Shira's story is an example for the rest of us."

After dinner, Shira drove me back to the Zulbergs'. She pointed out the picture from the cover of my book, *My Sister, the Jew,* which was posted on both sides of the street. As before, when we first started driving on the "wrong" side of the road, I had a feeling of the familiar and unfamiliar. My very familiar face — plastered all over the unfamiliar walls of South Africa!

Shira, ever practical, saw me looking at the posters and said, "We did a great job on the advertising, Ahuvah."

"Yes, I see." Odd. Where Shira saw only an advertising campaign, I saw a person misplaced in her ancestral continent. No matter how "familiar" Africa might be for me, I felt unfamiliar. For here I was, African in my origin, American in my upbringing — and totally Jewish in my heart's longings.

But whatever the symbolic meanings of my picture posted in South Africa, I had to admit that it worked as advertising, as Shira had said. The next morning Shira arrived punctually at 7:30 a.m., and I began a grueling day of running from one lecture to the other. I began with a lecture to a group of top business professionals in Johannesburg. Following the lecture they asked a variety of intellectually stimulating questions and also served refreshments. Too soon, Shira entered the room and said, "Ahuvah, we must leave immediately if we are going to make it to our next lecture on time."

The second lecture was at the Academy Girls' High School. As the introductions were made my attention shifted to the students who were anxiously waiting to hear my story. I thought about the many times in my career that I was the first Black woman to hold a position in a company; and here were all these young girls, about to see and hear the first Black Jewish woman they had ever met. Some things never change!

My leadoff story was my first visit to Israel, and my conclusion was the story of my first visit in an Orthodox shul, for Kol Nidrei. The girls had tears in their eyes when I finished. The bell rang for the next class, but they simply refused to go, hovering around me like a bird around its nest, still plying me with questions. Only when Shira announced that we would be late for my next lecture did they let me leave.

We drove at top speed to my next lecture, at Yeshiva College Girls' High School. We arrived without a moment to spare. Once again, talk and tears flowed together. I thought they were going to be more interested in my business background, but they seemed more interested in my spiritual journey. They wanted to know about my upbringing. They asked questions about my parents and grandparents as well as about my educational background. They were inquisitive about my adjusting to the Israeli lifestyle and its impact on my life. They laughed when my topic shifted from the seriousness of the *beis din* to my move to Bayit Vegan.

After the talk, there was just time for a quick lunch — but a quick lunch South African style means an entire steak dinner! Immediately after we were on the road again, this time to lecture at Bnos Bais Yaakov High School. The lecture was held at Chagall's Restaurant, in a shopping mall. Upon entering the mall, we were immediately surrounded by girls. They recognized me from the picture on my book cover and started talking to me. Some of them had already read my book. At one point the owner of Chagall's realized what all the commotion was about, and she came over to welcome me. She had also read my book and stated that she was honored to have me present.

Before my talk, there was a brief presentation by the girls to a *rebbetzin*, in honor of her completing tenure at their school. The accolades that the girls accorded her were unbelievable. Even I had tears in my eyes as they spoke so fondly of her boundless service and acts of *chesed*. After presenting her with a gift, they introduced me. I thought to myself, *What a difficult act to follow*. I decided to be up-front with the girls and began by telling them, "When I grow up, I want to be just like your *rebbetzin*." I was rewarded with the girls' friendly laughter, which gave me the confidence to continue with my lecture.

Seated after the lecture, with yet another wonderful meal placed in front of me, I began to answer the girls' questions. One girl asked me an intriguing question: "Ahuvah, do you mind if we call you Black?"

My answer to her was simple. "No, not at all. I am an African American Jewess."

And yet, the answer was really not as simple as that. I looked at the girls, with their pure *neshamos* — they were my sister Jews. But I also saw the African workers in the restaurant, who looked puzzled at the sight of a Black woman holding a room full of young White girls enthralled with her words. What relation did I have to them?

At the conclusion of my talk, one of the girls asked, "Ahuvah, do you think your mother and grandmother are proud of you?"

It was a question I had heard before, and I answered it as always, "Yes! Positively, they are."

And yet here, in South Africa, I realized that my relationship with my mother and grandmother, my Black family, was really more complicated. I thought about their struggles and realized that they had much in common with the struggles of the Black Africans. My grandparents had been hired workers living in shacks on a plantation, subsisting at the mercy of the plantation owners. They worked the land and got a portion of food and received minimal wages.

But my grandmother, may she rest in peace, was a God-fearing woman with a dream and boundless faith. She prayed to God for help with steadfast conviction that one day they would own their own property. Thank God, my grandfather worked extremely hard and saved his money. Eventually, he bought a farm of 125 acres and educated his children, all because of my grandmother's dream.

The most important thing to my grandmother was not to see her family free from the slavery of economic hardship, but to pass on her legacy of belief and prayer. Every night when I recite the bedtime Shema, I am transported back in my thoughts to my grandmother's commitment to prayer.

She dreamt that someday her children, grandchildren, and great-grandchildren would honor God in all their ways. That was her prayer throughout the years. On a spiritual level I believe that her fervent prayers were answered, because her granddaughter became a true *eved Hashem*.

And here I was in Africa, and my grandmother, through me, was still inspiring prayer; how she would have rejoiced to know that her life had inspired so many Jewish women, including me. Observing the faces of those young seminary students while sharing her story with them, I couldn't help noticing their look of awe about the greatness of my grandmother. A Black Baptist woman from Mound Bayou, Mississippi, married to a share-cropper, now has a granddaughter traveling all over the world inspiring Jews to daven, to pray.

And that, ultimately, explained to me my relationship to the Black Africans around me. Though they seemed so different to me — as strange as a car driving on the wrong side of the road — during my visit to South Africa, I experienced a soul reso-nance and began to relate more to my ancestors. And yet it is a relationship always tempered by my Jewish vision. On the one hand, the groans of a slave desiring to be free haunted me; on the other hand, the painful song of slavery that hums through my mind whispers the tune of the beautiful words in our Hag-gadah, "We were once slaves in Egypt." My heart cried out to Hashem for my Black African sisters and brothers who needed liberation, as the Torah states, "Is there anything too hard for God?" (*Bereishis* 18:14).

So my soul wept in South Africa, for the atrocities of the past and the hope for the future. My Black ancestors suffered; my Black grandmother believed; and my Jewish soul somehow combines suffering and belief to bring me to my own life jour-ney, my own *tafkid* in this world.

My Jewish sisters and brothers, I am so grateful that you are providing jobs and housing for your workers and treating them as decent human beings.

Before I fell asleep that night, my thoughts focused on the realization that my visit was a *tikun* and that perhaps my life journey was the actualization of my grandmother's prayers.

I felt like Alex Haley when he had traced his ancestry back to Africa and proclaimed, "I found you, you old African." I can also say I have found a link to an old African. But on a deeper level my spiritual roots transcend my African ones, going all the way back to Har Sinai. My voice echoed his words: "I found you, the *emes*." Now I know why I was born: to reach out to others and bring them close to Hashem.

Chapter Eight

Cape Town

fter a very full day in Johannesburg, I flew off to Cape Town. There I met Rabbi Yonason Shippel, who had arranged my lectures. As soon as I arrived, he took me to see the sights of the town.

The cable car started its ascent to Table Mountain. Apprehensive about looking downward, I focused my gaze on the top of the mountain. I thought to myself, *This has always been my goal in life: to reach for the top and not settle for second best.* As a Black child growing up within a White, male-dominated society in America, I had faith in God and truly believed that Black was beautiful. This sense of pride enabled me to maintain my dignity and overcome the stigma associated with being a Black woman, to succeed in college and as a professional. Thirty-two years in corporate America — as far as I was concerned, that was equivalent to a Ph.D.

I viewed each challenge along the way as an opportunity to break the chains that had shackled my ancestors. When I was blocked from success by some obstacle, I looked to the obstacle itself for the solution; the solution to overcome every trial was interwoven in the trial itself. Years later, I learned of a concept in Judaism that expresses this thought that I lived by: "Hashem has already prepared the remedy before the sickness."

Even at that time I viewed myself as a free woman, unhampered by prejudice. Before I could even say the words, I viewed myself as an *eved Hashem*, a servant of God. I saw all my personal accomplishments as a vehicle to overcome the stereotypes of ethnic profiling, with God's help. It was as if my *neshamah* knew that my redemption was forthcoming. So I anchored myself to the *emes* and stayed focused on the mountaintop. I saturated my upward journey with the word of God so that no man could enslave my mind, all praise be to Hashem!

So as I stood here on top of the most beautiful physical mountain I had ever seen, the words from my old life — "Free at last, free at last. Thank God Almighty, I am free at last" — mingled with the words from my new life — "I cast my eyes unto the mountains, from where will my help come? My help will come from God, Creator of the heavens and the earth...."

The trees and greenery that draped the slopes of the mountain were a deep emerald green, presenting an awesome contrast between the turquoise blue of the ocean and the lighter blue of the sky. As I stood awestruck at the view, Rabbi Shippel's voice broke the silence.

"Ahuvah, have you ever seen anything this exquisite?"

"Not in all my years of traveling. In all honesty it's the most magnificent view I've ever seen."

Rabbi Shippel started to describe the sights from the top of the mountain. His daughter, Chana Sarah, and I listened attentively. Devil's Peak and Lion's Head flanked Table Mountain to the left and Signal Hill formed an impressive backdrop to Cape Town on the right.

Rebbetzin Shippel had prepared sandwiches for us. We found a nice area to sit down and enjoy our tasty lunch. It was a long way from a gourmet Shabbos meal in Jerusalem to a picnic on Table Mountain, but Jerusalem was where my trip to the mountaintop had actually begun.

I had first met Rabbi Zechariah Sprung when he lectured on the parashah at Migdal Shul one Shabbos. *What an articulate speaker*, I thought as I sat there listening to his insights. He reminded me of the dynamic speakers we used to watch at our annual sales meetings. Certainly his Torah message was much richer, with more substance and depth than those sales pitches in my mind.

Soon after, I was delighted to receive an invitation to the Sprungs' home for Shabbos. I hoped that Rabbi Sprung's dinner conversation would be as inspiring as his more formal *divrei Torah*, and I was not to be disappointed. Not only did he have a great sense of humor, but he also had a unique style of presenting the Torah. He cited some of the leading sages of each generation, giving information about their lives and their contributions, as well as the historical period in which they lived. He had a way of drawing his listeners into the lives of the sages. I vividly remember this one particular story about the life and work of Rabbi Eliezer Silver.

"Rabbi Eliezer Silver, the head of the Orthodox rabbis of America, was a great scholar who studied in the world-renowned Yeshiva of Slobodka. He came to America in a time of great apathy during World War II. Jews in America were largely indifferent to the suffering of their Jewish brothers and sisters in the camps. Rabbi Silver was instrumental in recreating a proud Jewish identity in the United States. He was responsible for the march of five hundred rabbis in Washington, D.C., on the day before Yom Kippur in 1942. Afterwards President Franklin Delano Roosevelt refused to receive him and his delegation, and he publicly denounced Roosevelt as an anti-Semite. This incident reawakened Jewish identity and started the Vaad Hatzalah, which raised millions of dollars during World War II to save thousands of Jews. After the war Rabbi Silver went around the world inspiring and strengthening Jews. He was instrumental in bringing many Jews who had lost faith during the Holocaust back into the fold. He was a man of his time in every sense and left his imprint on one of the great watershed events of Jewry in America."

During dessert, the rabbi spoke about his *talmid* in Cape Town, Rabbi Yonason Shippel. He and his wife had lived in Bayit Vegan for a short time and then moved to Cape Town, where they had started a branch of Ohr Somayach in December 2000. At first, Rabbi Shippel could barely get a minyan of ten men for his Shabbos-only shul. Shortly after the word started to spread, and weekday minyanim began — and *baruch Hashem*, they have not missed a minyan since. They also opened the JLE (Jewish Learning Exchange) in Sea Point, which today has a thriving community.

Even after the Shippels moved to Cape Town, Rabbi Sprung and Rabbi Shippel continued their studies together by telephone for an hour each week.

After my Shabbos lunch at the Sprungs, Rabbi Shippel was just a name and a story to me. I never dreamt that I would meet him and his family. However, when Cape Town was added to my itinerary, the first person I called was Rabbi Sprung. He was elated and asked me to give Rabbi Shippel his warmest regards. And here I was, on the top of the mountain with Rabbi Shippel himself!

After my tour of Table Mountain, I headed to Loren Manors, a guest house where I was booked to stay for three nights. From the outside, the house looked like a plantation mansion in Atlanta or New Orleans. Inside, the decor was exquisite, as well. As soon as we walked in the owner came to greet us. "Welcome, Ms. Gray, we are so happy to have you visiting with us." Her English was impeccable and she introduced herself as Amanda Clark. She was a Black South African. I suspected that she was educated because of her elegant demeanor.

"Before I show you to your room, would you like a tour of our guest house?" she asked cordially.

"With pleasure," I answered. She proceeded to tell me that it had originally been a mansion, and it had been auctioned off. She had been sure that she couldn't afford the price, but miraculously it all worked out. As we started our tour, she escorted me into a lovely salon with a fireplace.

"If you have any guests you can entertain them here, Ms. Gray."

"It's gorgeous and I love the antique furniture."

"I bought all the furniture and did the decorating myself."

Next she escorted me to the dining room, where the table was already set. Each guest had his or her own sitting room, decorated tastefully with antique furniture. As we walked back to the entryway my feet sank into the beautiful Oriental rugs, and there were fresh flowers everywhere.

There were more lovely flowers lining the stairway which led to my room. When Amanda opened the door to my room, I couldn't believe my eyes. It was decorated in a lovely African motif and I had a chaise lounge and a beautiful view of the ocean.

Alone in my magnificent room, I peered out the window at the Atlantic Ocean, watching the waves break and wondering why Hashem had brought me here. Was there something here that I was supposed to learn, or something that I was going to teach?

Still uncertain, I went downstairs and began talking to Amanda. We both sat down; intuitively, I knew it was going to be a lengthy conversation. She wanted to know where I was from, and I asked her which university she had attended in America. I wasn't surprised to hear that she had attended Harvard University in Boston. She was an attractive, sophisticated woman with meticulous diction. Her daughter, a lawyer, lived in America.

"Ahuvah, it wasn't easy for a Black African woman to be married to a White South African. When I would answer the door, people used to ask for the mistress of the home. How shocked they would be when I would look them in the face and say, 'I am the mistress.' We couldn't go to restaurants together — not allowed. It was the most inhumane treatment I have ever experienced in my life."

I had read about apartheid in history books, but talking to one of its victims made it real to me. Amanda was lovely; concerned about my kosher food, careful to keep it all separate in the refrigerator — even the drinks. She offered her office phone for any calls and her own computer for my e-mails. Her past suffering had not made her bitter; indeed, perhaps her sensitivity to her guests' needs came in part from her own difficult past.

Amanda told me that the maid would see to anything I needed. I thanked her and went up to my room, where I started to unpack. Five minutes later, there was a knock on my door. A young Black woman came to my door with some hot water for tea — I had brought tea and coffee with me.

"Excuse me, missy," the young girl said quietly, "I hope I am not disturbing you. What can I do to help you?"

Holding back tears, I answered, "Thank you so much for the hot water. What is your name?"

"My name is Winny, missy."

"Winny, please call me Ahuvah."

"Yes, missy, whatever you say."

Realizing that I wouldn't be able to change her way of looking at herself and at me, I thanked her again. I told her there was no need for her to turn the bed down and gave her a tip.

As she walked out, I remembered the first time I visited my grandparents and my grandmother took us shopping in Memphis. When my grandmother paid the clerk she said, "Yes, sah."

Then the clerk asked if I wanted a lollipop and I said no. My grandmother apologized to him and told him I was from Chicago. He nodded his head and said he understood. Once we were outside she said to me, "Little Delores, you have to say, 'Yes, sah' and 'No, sah' to the white man, you hear."

I can't recall ever questioning anything my grandmother said, but in my childlike innocence I asked why. She replied, "Don't ask why, Delores. I will explain it to you when you're old enough to understand."

Well, it looks like that day will never come; I will never be "old enough" to understand why any finite human being, White or Black, thinks he has authority over another one of God's creations. Perhaps even at that tender age I knew all human beings were created *b'tzelem Elokim* — Winny or Amanda or me as much as any Southern White sales clerk!

When Winny closed the door I burst into tears. Even after she had been emancipated, the painful effects of being shackled had left this young woman maimed and scarred. I turned for comfort to *Tehillim*, quoting Psalm 90, "Lord, You have been an abode for us in all generations." I added my own silent prayer: "Oh God, I can't take it. She doesn't have to be a slave to me. Please break the chains that have this woman bound." I also took a moment for *hakaras hatov*, remembering with gratitude my parents, who taught us never to hate another human being or to look down upon anyone, even as they gave us the sense of our own worth that would not allow me to call another "missy" or "sah."

I took a deep breath, regained my composure, and recalled a lesson I had learned in seminary: The Meshech Chochmah, in his commentary to *Bemidbar* 11:28, writes that there are three individuals in the Torah that Hashem specifically calls "My servants" — Avraham, Kalev, and Moshe. These are the ones, he explains, who never addressed another human being as "my master" or who never said about themselves when speaking to another human being, "I am your servant." They only recognized Hashem as their Master, and they saw themselves as the servants of Hashem, but not of men.

I was scheduled for a lecture later that evening, and I knew a nap was the remedy I needed. Before dozing off, I started thinking about Alex Haley's *Roots* again and the horrible scenes of the slave ship he depicted. The thought that one of the slaves on the ship centuries ago was actually one of my ancestors was nearly unbearable. Once again, I wondered why Hashem had brought me here to Cape Town, to be reminded of such painful things. Then I thought that perhaps one reason was somehow to inspire the local African Blacks by sharing my experience, my strength, and my hopes with them. Perhaps seeing a Black American who had willingly chosen her Jewish path would let them know that they had the ability and the right to choose their path, as well. Moreover, perhaps they would pick up my sense that everything that occurred is from Hashem and that it's all for the good....

After my nap, Rabbi Shippel came to pick me up, and Amanda buzzed my room to inform me that he had arrived. I came downstairs to meet him. He told me that I would be speaking to the most influential group of Jews that lived in Cape Town and that their synagogue was thinking of breaking away from the Orthodox Union.

As we drove to the home where the lecture was going to be held, Rabbi Shippel pointed out different sights, but my mind was less on scenery and more on my teenage memories of listening to Martin Luther King and President Kennedy delivering their memorable speeches. I would go to my bedroom and repeat the speeches by heart. When I finished I would close out with a prayer, "God, I would like to be able to speak like that one day." As a child, I spoke with a lisp; I remember how discouraged I was, thinking that I would never be able to speak publicly, until I read the story of Moses, Moshe Rabbeinu, the greatest of our prophets and teachers, who spoke with a lisp as well. God doesn't need perfect diction in His messengers; perhaps, I had thought then to myself, perhaps someday I would have a message that God would want me to share with people as well. And here I was, in the land of my ancestors, about to give a message to my newfound people, to God's own nation.

Rabbi Shippel's voice brought me back to my present surroundings.

"This is the most affluent area in Cape Town. The wife in the family that we are going to is a convert, so your story should be extremely interesting to them. Do you have any idea of what you're going to say?"

"No! But don't get nervous. I never quite know what I am going to say until I see the group."

Rabbi Shippel replied, "If you're not nervous, then neither am I."

When we arrived Rabbi Shippel made all the introductions. Judging from the array of food, I thought it was going to be a large gathering, but as it turned out it was just three families, Rabbi Shippel, and myself.

Rabbi Shippel introduced me, and I began my story with the chapter in my book entitled "Harvard Conversion." The hostess was in tears throughout my talk, and the room was so silent I felt as if I could hear the tears slowly coursing down her cheeks.

When I finished, all the questions were about my conversion.

"Ahuvah, do you think that the Jerusalem Beis Din made your conversion too difficult?"

"No, on the contrary, I feel that the rabbis have every right to scrutinize us with extreme caution and make it difficult. In reality we don't have a clue what we are in store for until the conversion is completed. In my opinion the real test isn't the conversion process. It's how I live my life after I have accepted upon myself the 613 mitzvos."

"Ahuvah, did you ever think about doing a Conservative conversion?"

"No, I never considered any other conversion except Orthodox. I don't think we have any other levels of conversion. I simply wanted to do what was right in the eyes of God."

At the end of the question-and-answer session the hostess came over to me and told me that she appreciated and respected everything I said.

We spent the remainder of the evening eating hors d'oeuvres and making conversation. Soon Rabbi Shippel came over to me and indicated that it was time to depart.

Once we were in the car, Rabbi Shippel looked at me and said, "Do you know what just happened in that room?"

"No," I replied.

"The men in that room were contemplating breaking off from the Orthodox Union and adopting a less demanding type of conversion, more like Reform or Conservative. After listening to your lecture, they reached a unanimous decision to dismiss the idea."

"Rabbi Shippel, Hashem reversed the decision. I was just His messenger."

Back in the guest house, I had a snack and sat down to read a bit before falling asleep. My last thought before dozing off was a silent comment to God: *Hashem, I suppose this entire trip was preordained before I was born. You knew that You were going to send me, the granddaughter of a sharecropper, to South Africa to in-*

spire my Jewish sisters and brothers. Amazing! And with that, I
went to sleep after a very full first day in Cape Town.

Rabbi Shippel arrived punctually at 8:30 a.m. the next morning. I guess that "Jewish time" doesn't work in
South Africa! We went directly to a breakfast talk for the
women. There were approximately sixty women at the breakfast,
and the topic was prayer. The women seemed to enjoy the topic
and were very interested in the personal stories that I shared.

I focused the lecture on my praying grandmother, describing
how a visit to my grandparents' home at the age of forty-eight
changed my life, and I went home and committed my life to
prayer.

Everyone had tears in their eyes and so did I. I told them
how the Negro slave songs used to touch my *neshamah, lehavdil,*
just like the Shlomo Carlebach *niggunim* do today.

I had spoken at numerous gatherings already, and I could
anticipate most of the questions that would be asked at the end
of my talk. But there were still some surprises left — the last
woman who raised her hand asked me if I could sing a Negro
slave song for them. Rabbi Shippel had left the facility and
there were no other men present, so I sang a song I remembered
my grandmother singing: "Swing low, sweet chariot, coming for
to carry me home. Swing low, sweet chariot, coming for to carry
me home. I looked over yonder and what did I see? Coming for
to carry me home. A band of angels coming after me. Coming
for to carry me home."

I also told the women that Frederick Douglass, the famous
Black abolitionist, explained in his autobiography that when
Northerners heard slaves singing they assumed they sang from

happiness, though in reality slaves expressed their pain and fear in their haunting melodies. Now as I stood there looking at the women's faces I sensed that they had connected with the song as well and I felt a soul resonance with my South African sisters as well as with the blacks in South Africa.

I knew there were Torah reasons why we should have empathy for the past suffering of the Blacks in South Africa. During the 1920s, the Chafetz Chaim, a leading sage of that era who was then close to ninety years old, was heavily involved with the serious problems and dangers facing the Jewish people such as assimilation, the growing anti-Semitism in Poland and other European countries, the increasing poverty of Polish Jewry due to economic discrimination, and the campaign to destroy Judaism in Russia. During this difficult period, a rabbi who had returned from a trip to the Jewish community of South Africa came to visit the Chafetz Chaim. The Chafetz Chaim asked him, "What is the situation of the Blacks in South Africa?"

The rabbi, who was aware of the Chafetz Chaim's deep involvement with the serious problems of the Jewish people, asked the sage, "Why is the rebbe so concerned about the Blacks in South Africa?"

To which the Chafetz Chaim responded, "First, they are also people. Second, it says that eventually the entire world will be filled with the knowledge of God, which includes everyone, so shouldn't I be concerned with their welfare?" (Cited in the Kislev/November 5763 issue of the *Jewish Observer*.)

I was to remember the topic of songs two days later when I enjoyed Shabbos lunch at the Shippels in Cape Town. The Shabbos table was extended to its full size, as the hearts of my host and hostess were extended to all their many guests. We began with wonderful homemade challah, a festive array of salads, and traditional gefilte fish.

The conversation was lively as all the guests got better acquainted. Following the meal Rabbi Shippel and the men started singing some of the tunes of Shlomo Carlebach. One of them reminded me of a lovely story that Rabbi Yosef Hakohen had written about the melody.

When the men finished singing I shared the story that Rabbi Hakohen had written in one of his e-mail lessons. It was entitled "A Song of Comfort."

When I was fourteen, my first high school rebbe, Rabbi Zevulun Leib, taught our class how to serve Hashem with song. He was from the Yeshivah of Chaim Berlin, which had just produced a record titled, "Torah Lives and Sings." The *niggunim* on this record were composed by the yeshivah students and the great sage who headed the yeshivah, Rav Yitzchak Hutner. Rabbi Leib taught us these *niggunim*, as well as the *niggunim* that were composed by Rabbi Shlomo Carlebach. I was very sensitive to music, and when we would sing these deep and moving *niggunim* in class, I experienced a tremendous elevation of soul. Some of my friends, noticing my rapture, gently teased me, saying, "Yosef, you look like you've been transported to another world."

I really felt like I was in another world when my rebbe taught us those portions of the Talmud that were aggadah — stories and parables. He would chant the words of the aggadah to a haunting old *niggun* that some Torah students in Europe sang when they studied the aggadic portions of the Talmud. Through this *niggun* and other *niggunim* that our rebbe taught us, I began to truly feel that "Torah lives and sings."

There were a few *niggunim* that I especially loved, as they enabled me to express my deepest spiritual yearnings. One such *niggun* was composed by Rabbi Shlomo Carlebach to the following verse:

"Had Your Torah not been my delight, I would have perished in my affliction" (*Tehillim* 119:92, according to the Targum).

"Rabbi Shippel," I concluded, "that is the *niggun* that you just finished singing."

A Shabbos meal that began with my acquaintance of the Sprungs in Jerusalem and ended at the Shippels' home in Cape Town...songs of slaves, full of pain, and songs of our Sages, full of hope...how strange that in Africa, a land so far from my home yet so much part of who I was, my different lives seemed to be coming together. I remembered once again my tour of the mountaintop on my first day in Cape Town. Rabbi Shippel had given me a geography lesson on the top of the mountain. He explained that not far away was the Cape of Good Hope, where the Atlantic Ocean meets the Indian Ocean. At Cape Point, you could see where the currents of the two great bodies of water met, their different blue-green colors swirling and eddying together. Wasn't I like that, too — the convergence of so many lands and cultures and places in a swirling current with its own message and meaning?

My work was done in Cape Town. I left with many thanks and good-byes to the Shippels and flew back to Johannesburg for my final lecture.

Shira meet me at the airport. She was thrilled to hear a report of the lectures in Cape Town. We went to a dairy restaurant for lunch while I continued to tell Shira all the stories of my first visit to Cape Town.

Once we ordered our meals the owner of the restaurant came over to our table and introduced herself.

"Are you Ahuvah Gray?"

"Yes," I replied quietly.

"I want you to know I am saying *tehillim* every day because of your grandmother."

I thanked her and shared with her a few stories about my grandmother.

When she left, Shira looked at me and said, "What a *zechus* for your grandmother."

Later that evening, I went to my final lecture in Johannesburg. The auditorium was packed; there had to be over three hundred women and young girls present. Shira's mother and aunt were somewhere in the crowd. I decided to open with a heartfelt compliment about South African hospitality and then to have one of the girls read Shira's e-mail to me. I closed out my lecture by expressing my appreciation to Shira and her family and to the community in South Africa and shared with them the remarks of the owner of the restaurant: "I am saying *tehillim* every day because of your grandmother."

Somehow I felt that my grandmother had made this journey with me and had been totally liberated from her background as a sharecropper's daughter. She was a freed woman who had touched the lives of women all over the world because of her legacy of prayer and commitment to the words of King David.

May the legacy of King David live on as his lips continue to move in song even in the grave, as the Midrash states happens every time we quote *Tehillim*....

Before Shira's mother and aunt left they came behind the table where I was signing books and Mrs. Taylor gave me a hug with tears in her eyes.

"Thank you, Ahuvah."

"*Baruch Hashem*, Mrs. Taylor."

As Shira drove me back to my hosts that night, we didn't say good-bye. We just gave each other a big hug and said "*lehitraot*" — until the next time. When I said the bedtime prayer before drifting off to sleep, I thought about the closing words in Rabbi Hakohen's lesson on "A Song of Comfort"; truly my soul had been comforted by Jewish people in South Africa. "They will neither injure nor destroy in all of My sacred mountain, for the earth will be filled with knowledge of Hashem, as water covering the sea bed" (*Yeshayah* 11:9). How ironic that a girl named Shira, whose very name means song, had brought me to a land where the songs of my lives came together.

The words of the Torah have brought comfort, hope, and joy to seeking souls among all the peoples, including my enslaved African ancestors. As they studied and discussed the story of Israel's liberation from bondage, they gained new strength and faith that helped them to survive their own suffering and affliction. The Torah is more than "words"; the Torah is also a "song," as it is written: "Now write this song for yourselves" (*Devarim* 31:6). The Talmud explains that the "song" in this verse is referring to the entire Torah, which Israel is commanded to write (*Nedarim* 38a). The Torah is therefore a song of comfort, hope, and joy.

    May the freedom and the comfort that we experience as the Jewish people be shared by the entire world when Mashiach comes, and then we will all sing a new song.

Chapter Nine

If I Forget You, O Jerusalem!

huvah, Ahuvah, welcome home. How was your trip?"

"*Shalom*, Ezra. It was wonderful, and I am so grateful to be home."

Ezra, my taxi driver, picked me up at the airport. I was so happy to see a familiar face. After we placed the luggage in the car I filled him in on some of the details of my lecture tour.

As the taxi made the climb up the Tel Aviv–Jerusalem highway, I wondered what it must have been like during the time of the Temple, may it be rebuilt speedily in our days. I couldn't wait to get to Jerusalem. When I saw that sign that said "Jerusalem," I said, "Ezra, I love Jerusalem."

"So do I, so do I, Ahuvah."

As we made our ascent on the highway, my *neshamah* was ascending as well. I told Ezra to excuse me for just one moment so that I could quote one of my favorite chapters of *Tehillim*, Psalm 126:

"A song of ascents: When Hashem will return the captivity

of Zion, we will be like dreamers. Then our mouth will be filled with laughter and our tongue with glad song. Then they will declare among the nations, 'Hashem had done greatly with these.' Hashem had done greatly with us, we were gladdened. O Hashem, return our captivity like springs in the desert. Those who tearfully sow will reap in glad song. He who bears the measure of seeds walks along weeping, but will return in exultation, a bearer of his sheaves."

When I finished quoting the chapter in English, Ezra started quoting it in Hebrew and afterwards we both started laughing and crying at the same time. I returned to the holiest of cities to the sound of Ezra singing a *niggun* for Psalm 126.

We turned onto Rechov HaPisgah, a central street in Bayit Vegan. *Hapisgah* literally means "the height," and indeed I felt I had reached new heights in happiness and even ecstasy as I returned to my home. After unloading my things from the taxi, I wished Ezra *Shabbat shalom* and headed up the stairs.

Stepping out onto my balcony and breathing in the fresh clean air, I felt the atmosphere of physical and spiritual beauty filling my heart. My red and pink geraniums seemed to arch their green stems upwards towards the sky. *Baruch Hashem*, I was home.

Normally the first thing I do when I return from a lecture tour is unpack and do laundry. This time I just went straight to bed. Eight weeks away from home had exhausted me physically and spiritually. All that could nourish my soul was being in the holiness of Jerusalem and speaking to all the friends I had missed so much.

The next morning, I called my *abba* and *ima* first.

"Ahuvahleh, is that you? Abba, she's home."

I could hear Rabbi Heyman in the background. "The child should be *gebenched.*"

Next came a long round of questions. I answered as many as I could and looked at my watch. "I love you, Rebbetzin Heyman, but I have got to daven."

My davening was very sweet that day, but I was teary-eyed throughout. From my apartment I had the most spectacular view of the Knesset and the Shrine of the Book, as well as the minaret in the Old City. Even though the minaret blocked my view of Temple Mount, the significance of what it represents was engraved on my heart. The Temple Mount represents the return of the *Shechinah,* when Mashiach will come and the Temple will be rebuilt on that holy site.

My lecture tour to Hong Kong, Australia, and South Africa had been a tremendous *kiddush haShem,* judging from the responses of the audiences and newspaper reports. At the moment, however, I just wanted to regain my strength and nourish my weary soul. I had been away from the holiness of Yerushalayim for eight weeks, and I sat in my chair and wept. The tears I wept were not of sadness but, on the contrary, were tears of humility and gratitude. I was completely humbled at what God had helped me to accomplish and so grateful to be home. Despite having met warm, wonderful Jewish families around the world on my tour, being away from Jerusalem, my home sweet home, for so long was extremely difficult for me.

I knew it was a mitzvah to travel and share my story. The audiences seemed to receive *chizuk* from my words. And if I inspired even one person to daven a little better, didn't it make it worth my traveling to the far ends of the earth?

But it wasn't easy, nevertheless. Once while I was away, I

felt so distraught that I called Rebbetzin Heyman. I just wanted to talk to someone that was close to the *kedushah*. Rabbi Heyman answered the telephone and said his wife had just left the house. I asked him, "Why is it so painful to do a mitzvah? I am not complaining. The lectures are going very well. It's been a real *kiddush haShem*, but at the same time, I have never felt so spiritually drained in my life. Why do I have to sacrifice being away from my first love, Jerusalem, to do a mitzvah?"

Rabbi Heyman answered, "Ahuvah, you have just described what I often heard Rav Aharon Kotler, *zt"l*, state. He told me numerous stories of how difficult it is to do a mitzvah. He gave the following reason: When Moshe came down from Har Sinai with the first set of *luchos* with the Ten Commandments and God's holy letters engraved in them, he saw that the people had sinned with the golden calf. The tablets became heavy in his arm because the holy letters left, and he threw the tablets to the ground and broke them. Then he went back up to the mountaintop and fasted for forty more days and eventually brought down the second set of *luchos*. This set of *luchos* is the one that lasted. We see from here that Torah and mitzvos only come to us in this world through suffering and toiling."

I needed to hear the Torah spoken by someone with authority. Rabbi Heyman had just lightened the burden that was weighing so heavily on my soul. After speaking to him I felt a resurgence of inner strength.

Now, sitting on the chair in my living room, preparing for my first *shacharis* in Yerushalayim in two months, I thought about my mother, wishing that she were still alive. At this moment, I felt she was saying, "Go ahead, my little baby girl. I am right there with you. Everywhere you go I will always be with you." When she was alive, I felt there was no mountain too high for me to climb. Even if I stumbled and fell, Mother was there to pick me up. In almost the same heartbeat, I envisioned my granddaddy and grandmother smiling with pride for the child who had always loved God and had respected their teachings about honoring her elders.

But no matter how much I loved my family and was grateful for my upbringing, I had to leave them and their world for the seeds that they had planted within me to blossom. These were the thoughts that went through my mind before I started to daven.

As soon as I got to *"Adon Olam,"* I stopped crying. Avraham Avinu, the progenitor of our faith, comforted me. There was really no reason to cry. He was the first person to call Hashem *"Adon,"* Lord. He has been my main motivator throughout my life, and whenever I think of him, I receive *chizuk*. I feel a close connection to him as my forefather.

At that moment, the little Black girl who used to pretend that Abraham was her great-granddaddy was all grown up and sitting in her living room in Yerushalayim. Never had I sung *"Adon Olam,"* with such appreciation. I even sang it with the melody that we sing during the High Holidays. The *niggun* just sprang up from my soul. It was as if I was being transported into the future, to Yom Kippur, which was coming in two weeks.

I remembered what Rabbi Heyman had said at my book signing at the home of Elaine and Melech Lehman when *My Sister, the Jew* had first come out. Rabbi Heyman stated that if I wasn't the seed of Abraham, I wouldn't be able to say, "Blessed are You...God of our forefathers, God of Avraham, God of Yitzchak, and God of Yaakov," which I, like every other *frum*

Jew, say in the *Amidah* prayer three times a day. The Torah states, "Now Avraham was old, well on in years, and Hashem blessed Avraham with everything" (*Bereishis* 24:1), and "I have made you [Avraham] the father of a multitude of peoples" (ibid. 17:5). Our Sages say based on these two *pesukim* that every *ger* automatically becomes Avraham's child. Therefore when the convert prays, he or she can say "the God of our forefathers." The halachah that I could say these words puzzled me for years. Only when I heard those words of Rabbi Heyman did I understand. I really was a true daughter of Avraham.

As I continued to pray and focus on God's goodness, I no longer felt drained. I knew that the only way that I could nourish my soul on this level was with the *kedushah* of Jerusalem. As the verse says, "If I forget you, O Jerusalem, let my right hand forget its skill" (*Tehillim* 137:5). I also realized that the reason I am always enervated when I return home from a lecture tour is that I am unable to replenish my soul outside of Jerusalem.

Continuing with my intense prayers, I said *Birkas HaTorah*, the blessings of the Torah. Now I had arrived at *Birkas Kohanim*, the blessing of the priests. In my mind's eye, I remembered my first visit to the Kosel during the priestly benediction. At the time it seemed to me to be a vision, a reflection, of what the world will be like when Mashiach comes. The *kohanim* stood wrapped in their white *talleisim*, prayer shawls, in the first row next to the Kosel. They faced countless rows of Jews who stood with reverence and awe, receiving the blessing. There were people from all over the world with diverse backgrounds — a mixed multitude. But they all came because they were seeking the *emes*. This is what it will be like when Mashiach comes. The entire world will recognize the One and Only God. When we recite this *berachah* at home or at shul every day, we are, in a sense, remembering what will take place when the Temple service is reinstituted.

I also recalled having learned in seminary that the reason the section of *Birkas HaTorah* were instituted in our morning davening is that Moshe made a *berachah* before he read the Torah. So did Ezra the Scribe and the high priest on Yom Kippur. Every morning each Jew can connect with the *neshamos* of our greatest leaders through blessing and through Torah.

Now my soul was at peace. I had been feeding my *neshamah* with every word I uttered, and it was truly nourished, as my body is after I have eaten a nutritious meal. I was satisfied.

I was moved to tears once again when I read in Hebrew the words that changed my life: "My God, the soul You placed within me is pure." I finished these words and moved gracefully into the fifteen *berachos* called *Birchos HaShachar*. I say all those benedictions except for the one that says: "Blessed are You, Hashem, our God, for not having made me a gentile." Rabbi Heyman looked up the halachah and told me I should not say it, as it refers to one's state at the time of one's birth.

When I finished the fifteenth *berachah* I was ready for the *Akeidah*, the verse of the Binding of Yitzchak. I love davening the *Akeidah* because I realize that if I merit it, my requests of God will be answered in the *zechus* of the *Akeidah*. By the time I got to the beautiful words at the closing of the *Akeidah*, I felt as though I had had a *seudah* for the soul:

"What are we? What is our life? What is our kindness? What is our righteousness? What is our salvation? What is our strength? What is our might? What can we say before You, Hashem, our God and the God of our forefathers? Are not all the heroes like nothing before you, the famous as if they had never existed, the wise as if devoid of wisdom, and the perceptive as if devoid of intelligence? For most of their deeds are desolate and the days of their lives are empty before you. The preeminence of man over beast is nonexistent, for all is vain."

All is vain — but not for a Jew, who, through the study of Torah and the observance of mitzvos, can be part of the chain that began with the *avos*, the forefathers, and can connect with Hashem and His plan for our world. Through the mitzvos, through our prayers, and through the study of Torah we gain merit in the everlasting World to Come. And in revealing this message to the world through our studies, our prayers, and our actions, we, the Jewish people, are *kohanim*, priestly teachers, to all the nations. I felt so grateful to have been given the chance to become part of the chosen people, to add my study, prayer, and action to the nation of priests, and especially to have had the opportunity to share our message in the far reaches of the world.

But most of all, I was grateful to be home and to be a recipient of the peace that can only be experienced in Jerusalem.

"If I forget you, O Jerusalem, let my right hand forget its skill."

Spiritual Journeys

Chapter Ten

From Mississippi to Sinai to Jerusalem

ong Kong. Melbourne. Johannesburg. Cape Town.

For whatever reason He might have, God has allowed me to take my message to the farthest reaches of the world.

But perhaps before one can bring a message to those living in a distant land, the message must be honed much closer to home. My own message was cultivated in my native America and grew to fruition in my beloved adopted land of Israel.

But my message was originally planted in the one "place" closest to me — within myself.

One night, before dozing off to sleep in my apartment in Bayit Vegan, I saw a picture of myself as a child at my grandmother's, watching her as she prayed fervently. In the next scene I was an adult praying at the Kosel. In a matter of seconds, I was back in the South at my grandmother's, observing her acts of kindness to those confined to bed. These shifting images of being a little child and becoming an adult repeated themselves. The only thing the little child within me didn't comprehend was how I could hopscotch from Mississippi to Jerusalem so rapidly.

When I was a child visiting my aging grandparents in Mississippi, I had never imagined that I would ever go to the Sinai Desert. The place was a myth, a story, not a real place for a real person.

But when I grew up, I found my path to my own reality took me to a mythic place, to the Sinai that I had heard tell of as a child. I went on a spiritual as well as a physical journey to Sinai. I had no idea where the quest would lead. At the time Christianity and Judaism waged a raging battle within me. Ultimately, the search for my true identity took me far from my spiritual and physical roots in Mississippi to my new home, Jerusalem.

But though the search took me far from Mississippi, Hashem enabled me to transplant the seeds of prayer and kindness that I saw in my grandmother. I learned that these are the cornerstones of a Jewish life. Rooted in Jerusalem, I hoped they would grow and blossom.

The inner yearning that caused my soul to wander through its dry and crooked places for so many long and agonizing years reached its peak in the Sinai Desert when my soul finally returned to its true spiritual origin. It was there, in that dryness, that I became saturated with the truth. With the help of God, I rediscovered the peace that had been eluding me for so many years. Every Jewish soul was present on its highest level of spirituality in that desert when the Torah, the Divine teaching, was given to us. I thanked the Almighty for my own desert experience that led my soul to reconnect to its true spiritual roots at Mount Sinai and beyond to my true home, Jerusalem, the city of God.

Once the word spread about my story — an African American minister who had found her way to Judaism — I began lecturing in Jerusalem. One day I received a telephone call from a woman who identified herself as Rachel Nadel. She wanted me to lecture for a seminary called Michlelet Esther, a division of Neve Yerushalayim located at the time in the Jerusalem neighborhood of Kiryat Moshe. They had a group of approximately forty post–high school girls from modern backgrounds in a one-year program.

Two weeks later I took the number 16 bus from Bayit Vegan to Michlelet Esther. The first person to greet me was Rachel Nadel, who said that the girls were extremely excited to hear me speak.

I began my story by focusing on davening. I spoke about my grandmother and her strong commitment to prayer. I told them how I learned the twenty-third psalm on my grandmother's lap when I was just four years old. As I spoke to the girls, the thought entered my mind, *I wonder when was the first time I prayed.* This question haunted me and I had to struggle to stay focused and not lose my train of thought.

At this point, I started to share with the girls anecdotes about my conversion. "When I walked into the Beis Din HaGadol in Jerusalem five years ago, I didn't know what to expect. But I knew Hashem was with me every step of the way. So I quoted in my mind several of my favorite verses of *Tehillim*, 'My Lord, You

have been an abode for us in all generations.... Teach us to
count our days, and we shall acquire a heart of wisdom.'

"I stood in front of those judges in suspense, not knowing if
they were going to turn me away again or not. After what seemed
an eternity of silence Rabbi Eliyahu Bakshi-Doron, then the
Chief Sephardic Rabbi of Israel, said, 'Ms. Gray, we will be getting back to you in few days.' I breathed a sigh of relief and left,
feeling hopeful. But I didn't stop there. I called that administra-
tive office three or four times every day, and finally after the
third day the rabbi, sounding exasperated, said, 'Ahuvah, you
are a Jew. You can pick up your papers tomorrow.'

"When I hung up that telephone I started singing, 'Thank
You, Hashem, thank You. I just want to thank You, Hashem.' "

I finished the story with my favorite detail, describing how
after I went to the *mikveh* with my friend Natanella, Natanella's
five-year-old, Avraham Moshe, said to his mother, "Ima, why is
Ahuvah still Black?"

I concluded the lecture with the description of the *seudah*
that Nishmat gave in honor of my conversion. As I thought
about that *seudah* more intently I realized that it was a *seudah*
for my soul. We dined in splendor and magnificence. The
Nishmat students and staff prepared the food themselves, but
it was Hashem who set that table that day. All the elements of a
delightful gourmet meal were there in honor of my conversion.
For me, it was the ultimate birthday party, celebrating my re-
birth as a Jew.

At the conclusion of the lecture the young girls seemed ap-
preciative and were anxiously waiting for the question-and-
answer period. To my surprise, the majority of their questions
were about prayer.

"Ahuvah, how can I learn to love davening like you do? I find it boring and my mind wanders all over the place. Besides, it takes me so long to daven in Hebrew, and I don't even know what I am saying. I think it's a complete waste of time. Is there any advice you can give to help us concentrate better?"

Before answering the questions, I gave them some deep thought. As I was formulating my thoughts, the answer to the question that had come to me earlier that evening flashed clearly in my mind's eye, and I remembered the first time I had prayed to God.

I must have been five years old at the time. I was already well acquainted with God as a shepherd and the keeper of the flock. But I wanted to know where His dwelling place was. The first words that I uttered to God were, "Dear God, where are You out there?"

I remember that feeling of certainty that God existed, even though I didn't know His domain. The memory of my certainties and of what prayer meant to me helped me formulate answers to the girls' difficult questions.

"To daven with *kavanah*, concentration, takes years of practice. Various circumstances in my life have demanded that I give prayer my most scrupulous efforts; my commitment to prayer has developed after many years of hard labor. You can practice praying the same way. Just start with ten minutes and keep going until you attain more concentration, even if it takes more time. When I first started davening in Hebrew it took me four hours. Several months later I had decreased the time to one-and-a-half hours. I am sure it will work for you as well. I had to learn how to harness my thoughts to prevent my mind from wandering all over the place. When my mind would start to wander, a *passuk* from *Yeshayah* or *Tehillim* would come to my mind and get me back on track. It takes years of practice and discipline."

The last statement the girls made took me by surprise: "You should be teaching us about prayer."

Before I left, I thanked the girls for such a stimulating hour. One of them, Malka Albert, offered to carry my briefcase and walk me to the bus stop.

Four days after the lecture, immediately after I finished morning davening, my telephone rang. It was Rachel Nadel. "Ahuvah, you won't believe this, but all the girls have been getting up to daven *shacharis* every day. Several of them also went to the principal, Rabbi Baruch Smith, and asked him if you could teach a *tefillah* class." I listened with sheer jubilation as she continued, "Ahuvah, are you still there?"

I was speechless with joy and surprise, but I forced myself to answer with a simple, "Yes."

Rachel continued, the excitement in her voice almost making the telephone wires jump. "We've never seen anything like this. Rabbi Smith asked me to call you to determine when you could start and how much you would charge. It's not final as of yet, but he just wanted to see if it was within our budget. I will have a definite answer for you within a week. If I were you, Ahuvah, I'd start preparing a syllabus to submit to Rabbi Smith. Do you know that the girls haven't stopped talking about you since you left? Is it okay to give out your telephone number, because they want to come for Shabbos?"

"Yes, please do," I managed to utter.

As soon as I hung up the telephone, my voice returned in

force. I started shouting, "I don't believe it! Is this really real?" I started laughing and couldn't stop. My jubilation subsided a bit when I realized the implications of that phone call. "Oh my goodness, what am I going to teach?"

As I nervously grabbed the telephone to call Rebbetzin Heyman, I thought, *Hashem, please have mercy on me. I am going to need Your help!*

When I told the *rebbetzin* she was more nervous than I was.

"What are you saying? What are you going to teach them? What about your Hebrew?"

"Don't worry, I will let them read the Hebrew because their Hebrew is better than mine."

As I hung up the telephone, I knew she had very real concerns. Oh, how I wished I was an expert in everything. Me, teach the prayers of our Holy Tongue — I could barely hold a conversation with my *makolet* owner about the weather or the price of a bag of milk without making a grammar mistake! The perfectionist voice within me cried out, *Oh! Why hadn't I been born a Jew who had been able to attend Hebrew school at an early age? Could it be that God has given me a job here without giving me the necessary tools to succeed at it?*

I did what I so often do when I feel overwhelmed with questions. I called Rabbi Hakohen. I knew he would have a scholarly approach and I was hoping that some of his wisdom would rub off on me. We learned in seminary that a *kohein* has a special *neshamah*. I have always listened to Rabbi Hakohen because he speaks with the wisdom of the elders. He draws on the insights that he gained from his study of Torah, including the Midrashim, to give brilliant advice.

When I told Rabbi Hakohen my dilemma, these were his

wise words. "You see, Ahuvah, you're going to be using the skills that you grew up with. In addition, you will find Torah sources on prayer. Don't worry about the Hebrew. Your gift is that you speak from your heart. What comes from the heart reaches the heart."

As he spoke those words I recalled the verse in *Tehillim*, "Hashem is close to all who call upon Him — to all who call upon Him sincerely" (*Tehillim* 145:18). Somehow from the deep reservoir of Hashem's love this teaching experience was bestowed upon me to further develop my ability to daven.

Rabbi Hakohen gave me the confidence to go ahead with the idea, but I was still faced with one overwhelming question: *What in the world was I going to teach?* I desperately needed a lesson plan.

I spent the whole day contemplating my preparation for the lesson. The following morning while I was reciting *Ashrei* in the morning prayers, as soon as I quoted the *passuk*, "You open Your hand and satisfy the desire of every living being," the idea came to me in a flash: Chanah's prayer.

I have always been fascinated by the story of that noble woman. Actually, she was the subject of one of the sermons I had given in my early years as a minister. However, I didn't learn the true essence of Chanah's life until I studied in seminary. In the Jewish commentaries, I discovered the most important details. We learned that Hashem closed Chanah's womb so that she would pray and become the Chanah that we know, the mother of the Prophet Shmuel. Sometimes all of us need some tough circumstances to push us to prayer. Even the provocation of Peninah, which caused Chanah great pain, was

God's will. Peninah was punished for her behavior in the end, but only because she carried her actions beyond what was permitted by Hashem.

I had often wondered about the painful circumstances in the lives of those two women. If life's challenges were there to fuel prayer, what might it mean for me? Could it be that my delay in discovering Judaism was because my commitment to prayer needed to be more fully developed, like Chanah's? Fully realizing, of course, that I was not on the level of Chanah, I was still intrigued by her life for many years and strived to develop my prayers more fully as she had done.

At breakfast, I remembered the dream I had had about hopscotching from Mississippi to Jerusalem. As a child my grandmother had been my main role model for prayer. As I grew older Chanah became one of my main inspirations. That's why I was so excited to share this part of my inner prayer life with the students at Michlelet Esther. My worlds were merging in such a beautiful way and my prayer life was evolving. "Oh God! Help me focus my attention on the most pressing issues — like working on my lesson plan for the *tefillah* class."

After spending the entire day trying to construct a syllabus for teaching Chanah's prayer, from the first book of *Shmuel*, I finally found the material that I needed. It had taken several hours to search through several folders, and I eventually developed a lesson plan based on the ideas that Simi Peters had taught in a *navi* class at Nishmat.

The final approval for the class came a few days later, on *motza'ei Shabbos*. Rachel Nadel called and arranged for the class to be taught weekly on Wednesdays. All they needed was for me to fax a copy of the syllabus to them. The girls had voluntarily given up their free time for the class.

When the taxi dropped me off on that first Wednesday, Rachel was there to meet me and with her usual enthusiasm took me directly to Rabbi Smith's office. "Be *matzliach*, Ahuvah," he said, "and hurry, the girls are eagerly awaiting."

Rachel and I ran directly to the library, where the girls were already seated. I had not anticipated such a large crowd, so Rachel had to make more copies of the syllabus.

The first three classes we basically followed the syllabus. During that time I noticed that the girls were really more interested in true stories of how I had developed my prayer life.

I shared with them how my first concept of God was that He was a shepherd, herding a large flock of people. But my biggest concern was where He lived. Soon I figured out that it was somewhere far beyond in the sky and it really didn't matter as long as He was there.

My second recollection of praying was when I asked God if He was real. Even at this early age I felt that He answered my prayers. Not verbally, but in my heart I instinctively came to know He was real.

After feeling confident that He existed my next question was, "Does He love me?" This one was tougher; it took me many years to find an answer to this question. It came to me one Mother's Day when I was already an adult. I always attended services with my mother on that day.

The pastor's text that day was "The Virtue of a Mother's Love." Throughout my life I knew my mother loved me because she expressed her love through her actions and deeds. But I was still plagued by the problem of how to equate the love of God to my mother's love. Surely He couldn't love me as much as she did?

The answer came from that country preacher that day. It wasn't an eloquent sermon, but God opened my heart to receive the message that day. The preacher simply said, "If a mother could love a child so dearly, how much more is God's love?"

I cried during his sermon because I knew my mother loved me. But when I left that place that day I knew that Hashem's love surpassed my mother's love. Up to that point I didn't think there was any greater love than my mother's love for her children, but there was!

On the bus ride back home after that first class, I thought to myself, *Maybe that dream wasn't so childish after all.* I never put much credence in dreams, but that last one might have had some truth in it. Perhaps when I was a little girl visiting my aging grandparents in Mississippi, I was directed by God. Who knows, maybe the spiritual backdrop of my grandmother's life was my preparatory course for the ultimate classroom at Michlelet Esther. On a spiritual level, I believe that I really did complete that journey. Even though it seemed a bit impossible to travel from Mississippi to the Kosel as a child, in reality I was destined to make that journey as an adult.

One of the great benefits of my class was getting to know the girls better. We developed a strong bond in that room. During our numerous conversations the girls would say, "Ahuvah, you have no idea how much you inspired us to daven."

I never thought much of the depth of their statement until

that class ended. Not only had my teaching inspired them, but I too was revitalized. I am so grateful to Hashem for allowing me this opportunity for growth. Teaching that *tefillah* class was a life-changing experience for me. It gave me a deeper appreciation for the role models that Hashem placed in my life. And seeing how much went into preparing even one class gave me a new respect for the erudition and efforts of all my many teachers.

My *tefillah* purified me as well. I remember walking down the street in Bayit Vegan and meeting a lady who davens at my shul, HaGra. She said, "You know, you don't look the same as you did when you first moved into this neighborhood."

I agreed with her immediately.

The day after each class I felt a resurgence and determination to daven better than I ever had before. I felt a responsibility toward each girl in that room to be more deeply committed to prayer.

My prayer life took on new meaning at that point. I rooted my davening in the simple imagery that I had as a child, that Hashem was my shepherd, and ultimately His love for me is my primary motivation to daven and to daven some more. My understanding of the *tefillos* and my feelings about my teachers and my students developed that simple image and made it grow.

What developed as a result of my deep concentration is that I started to experience a synchronization of my thoughts while davening in Hebrew because I had memorized sections of the prayers in English. When I came to the parts that really spoke to my *neshamah* I would pause a moment and let the English words come into my mind.

Months passed and I had completed another lecture tour. My first day home I got a telephone call from Malka Albert, the girl who had walked me to the bus stop after my very first lecture. Malka had visited me several times on Shabbos, and we had grown close.

"Ahuvah, *mazal tov*, I am a *kallah*. Thank you so much for teaching me to daven with more *kavanah* for my *bashert*."

"Malka, I am so happy for you. *Mazal tov*! Does Rebbetzin Heyman know? She will be elated when she finds out that another one of her *kinderlach* is starting her home!" I felt like Malka was my spiritual child.

"Much have I learned from my teachers, more from my colleagues, but most from my students..." (*Pirkei Avos*). Malka Albert Zwick is now a wife and mother. She, her husband, and son live in Telz Stone. Now I know what *Yiddishe nachas* means!

When I mentioned to Malka that I was writing about our *tefillah* class, she asked if she could share with the readers what she had gained from those sessions. When she sent me her comments, I started to cry.

"And Rus clung to her [Naomi]" (*Rus* 1:14). A person's greatness comes from clinging to great people. When Ahuvah came to speak at Michlelet Esther, I saw such a special, pure person. I wanted to have a *kosher* with her, so I walked her to the bus and asked her for her phone number. I knew she had so much to give. A few other girls and I spoke with Rabbi Smith and he arranged for her to teach a class on *tefillah*.

Learning from her was one of the greatest experiences I merited to have. I remember that she knew most of *Tehillim* by heart and would quote many *pesukim*. She would show us beautiful and deep interpretations of *tefillah*. Learning *tefillah* from Ahuvah added so much *kavanah* to my *tefillos*. I feel that this is one of the most special connections that I have sought out, for I have clung to her greatness.

Just prior to departing for a lecture tour to London and Gibraltar, I was going for my daily walk in Bayit Vegan, thinking of Malka Albert's beautiful words. As I turned the corner by Boys' Town Orphanage, a lady stopped me.

"Excuse me, Ahuvah, but do you ever feel kind of empty and devoid of spirituality? Do you sometimes feel like your prayers are perfunctory?"

I looked at her with deep concern, for she seemed so sincere.

"No, I don't. I love davening and I have a legacy of prayer warriors — people who were committed to prayer — in my family."

"That's wonderful, Ahuvah. But it doesn't always happen like that for us who are *frum* from birth."

I listened with deep compassion as she continued, "This morning, I got up at 6:00 a.m. to daven, and then the baby started crying and then I had to get the other kids up and prepare breakfast and get them off to school. By the time I finished, I had no desire to finish davening. I feel so guilty. Is there any advice you can give?"

I put my hand on her shoulder and said, "Please don't compare yourself to me. It's not fair. You should realize that my personal circumstances are totally different from yours. I don't know what I would do if I had a household of children to take care of. My davening would fall apart!

"Hashem has graced me with the circumstances that allow

me to devote myself to this spiritual *avodah*, to growing through prayer. I consider it a privilege. Sometimes we have close friends and we can talk to them for hours. Sometimes we just have a few minutes and we call up to say, 'Hello, I love you!' You can do that with Hashem. Talk to Him all day. Hashem gave you a family to take care of. All the mitzvos you do in essence are your prayers."

She looked at me with tears in her eyes. "Thank you so much, Ahuvah."

Chapter Eleven

Lessons in *Emunah*

*J*anuary 27, 2002: Normally I don't listen to the English news at 1:30 p.m., but I had a feeling that I should turn it on that day. I sat in a chair motionless as I listen to the report. A female suicide bomber had blown herself up across from Sbarro's, a pizza shop in the center of Jerusalem. I sat there motionless, trying to take in the news.

Just five days before a gunman had shot and killed two people and wounded numerous others; one of the wounded was a student from Neve Yerushalayim named Sharon Dennis.* We were still davening for her, saying *Tehillim* around the clock.

Now, at a shoe store not far from Sbarro's Pizza, a suicide bomber had murdered fifteen people and injured one hundred and thirty others. Among the injured were the Sokolows, a family that was visiting their daughter in a seminary. The father, Mark Sokolow, had survived the September 11 attack on the World Trade Center, five months earlier, unscathed. He and his daughter were taken to Shaare Zedek Hospital and were

* Not her real name.

recuperating down the hall from one another. Afterwards the reporter said to Mr. Sokolow, "I think Someone up there is watching over you."

As soon as I heard the news, I immediately davened *minchah*. I was scheduled to give a lecture at Bnos Torah Seminary, but I didn't know what to say on such a day, in such a time of pain. At the moment I could have used some encouragement myself, yet I was moments away from giving a lecture that was supposed to inspire and encourage others.

During the spontaneous part of the prayer I asked Hashem to give me the tongue of the learned to speak a word in season to these young girls.

There were approximately sixty girls present as well as staff members. I began the lecture with the terrible story of the female suicide bomber. We read a couple chapters of *Tehillim* and I opened up with a story about my grandmother praying and how that affected my life. When we got to the question-and-answer session, they had lots of questions:

"Ahuvah, what was it like to make the transition from Christianity to Judaism?"

"What was the thing that you found the most difficult in Judaism?"

"Do you think anyone else in your family will become Jewish?"

I answered the questions one at a time. They were all familiar to me.

At the end of the lecture, the dorm counselor said, "Ahuvah, what thought would you like to leave the girls with today?"

I replied, "The decisions that you make today will determine your future. They will affect your children and grandchildren.

The world is watching you. Everything that you do in life should be a *kiddush haShem* — a sanctification of God's name.

"When I was in the eighth grade there was a Jewish dress Shop in my neighborhood called Jaynette's Dress Shop. It was located on Pulaski Road. I used to take the long way home from school every day to go by that dress shop. One day I got the courage to go into the shop and ask if they needed a worker. The owners hired me on the spot. I became very close to that family. I even used to visit them for Shabbos. When I was on the bus going to their home as a fourteen-year-old Black girl, I remembered reading in the Bible that the Jews were the chosen people. When I used to see religious Jews, I would look at them and say to myself, 'These people are holy.' I had read it in the Bible with my grandmother when I was a little girl in Mississippi.

" 'Delores, the Jews are the chosen people,' Grandmother would say.

"Perhaps you girls don't particularly want to be chosen. But you must know that the eyes of the world are on the Jewish people, on the land of Israel, and on Jerusalem.

"Today Hashem unified our prayers through tragedy and sorrow. This should cause us, the Jewish people, to cry to Him more than ever that He will hear our *tefillos* and bring us the ultimate joy!"

I left the school feeling grateful. I don't know who benefited more from that lecture, the girls or me. It was comforting and uplifting to be with them. Somehow I felt that by sharing my experiences, I was contributing to the continuity of the Jewish people. With murder and terror around us, we were affirming eternal life.

That Shabbos, some people I was eating lunch with mentioned that they wanted to walk down to
Shaare Zedek Hospital to visit the Sokolow family. Although
they didn't know the Sokolows, they thought the family would
appreciate visitors. I asked if I could join them. Who knew —
perhaps I could find some words to comfort these people who
were facing such pain.

We stopped at the front desk and they gave us the room
number. The family was on the tenth floor. The mother was ly-
ing in bed with her leg in a cast. Mr. Sokolow and his young
daughter were standing at her bedside. After we introduced ourselves, I gave Mrs. Sokolow an autographed copy of my book.

"Thank you, Ahuvah. I had wanted to purchase your book,
but I guess Hashem arranged for us to meet this way instead. It
will be much more interesting to read the book now that we
have met."

"My prayer is that you will enjoy it and that it will
strengthen you."

Her older daughter put in, "Everyone in my seminary is
reading your book, Ahuvah."

My friends and I were very touched by our visit with them
and felt it was a real privilege to meet them. Before we left
Mr. Sokolow suggested that we go say good Shabbos to
Sharon Dennis, the injured Neve girl, who was directly
upstairs.

As we walked up one more flight of stairs, I reflected with
amazement on the calm resolve of the Sokolow family. They
had an inner strength and peace about them and there was not
a trace or hint of any anger in any member of the family. In fact,
Mr. Sokolow said as we were leaving, "We're not going to take

our daughter out of seminary, and my family will be back in Eretz Yisrael again soon."

As my friends and I walked into the room of the Neve student I couldn't believe my eyes. The lovely girl was sitting up in bed, laughing and talking to a friend. When we introduced ourselves I told her that I was an alumni of Neve, and the Sokolow family had told us that she was here. I also mentioned that her story was a miracle, no doubt due to the *Tehillim* being said around the clock for her. I didn't want to mention too many of the details because I wasn't sure of how much of the story she knew, but I remembered hearing that the ambulance driver reported that she wasn't breathing when they first picked her up. The shot had penetrated one of her lungs. The more the ambulance crew worked on her, the more futile their efforts seemed. But miraculously she started breathing again, and she was now on the road to recovery.

Sharon thanked us for coming and motioned for us to sit down. She was very pleasant and simply talked about how happy she was that she would be going home in a few days.

As my friends and I began our walk back to Bayit Vegan, we discussed what we had gained from the experience.

"Have you ever seen anyone display as much strength as the Sokolow family and the Neve student did, Ahuvah?"

"No, I haven't. What I think is amazing is that neither the Sokolow family nor the student seemed to carry any anger against God in their hearts. The *emunah* and *bitachon* they have is amazing."

I learned some valuable lessons that Shabbos. Visiting the Sokolows and Sharon Dennis strengthened me and my *emunah*, faith in Hashem, which made my davening even stronger.

Chapter Twelve

A Song in My Heart

*E*very human being has a moment in time when his *neshamah* wants to break out in *shirah*, in song. My mind had often contemplated the true meaning of this desire. After studying and researching the topic and asking numerous rabbis and Torah scholars about it, I found that the answer was quite complex. "*Shirah* is the expression of the realization, recognition, and great appreciation of God's presence in the universe, when Hashem's created beings transcend in space and time and praise Him for His splendor and magnificent acts," Rabbi Heyman told me. I especially related to the idea that a person can come to his own *shirah* by recognizing the greatness of Hashem.

There are portions in the Torah where the words are actually *shirah*, meant to be sung. Perhaps the most famous *shirah* in the Torah is the "Song at the Reed Sea" (*Shemos* 14:30–15:19), by Moshe and the *bnei Yisrael*. Other songs of the Torah include the "Song of Miriam's Well" (*Bemidbar* 21:17) and the "Farewell Song" of Moshe (*Devarim* 32:1–43). In the Books of the Prophets there is the song Yehoshua sang after the miracle of the sun, Devorah's song of victory, and the "Song of Chanah." Chapter 92 in *Tehillim*, "A Song for the Sabbath Day," was composed by Adam in honor of the first Shabbos. The "Song of David" (*Shmuel* II, ch. 22) is followed in history by the greatest of all songs, the "Song of Songs" by Shlomo. The culmination of all these songs will be the song that will be sung in the Messianic age (see *Yeshayah* 30:29).

Although we cannot possibly compare ourselves to these greatest of spiritual giants, each one of us, on an individual level, has the capacity to recognize Hashem's wonders, to relate to His Divine providence, and to experience moments of joyous song.

My personal *shirah* came when my first family member came to Israel to visit me. Even though it is no comparison to the splendor of the songs written about in the Torah, my sister's visit struck a deep chord in my soul that caused my heart to spring forth in song.

Even though my parents hadn't made the journey during their lifetimes, my sister, Nellie, was scheduled to arrive in Israel for a two-week visit in February 2000, on a pilgrimage tour led by Dr. Charles C. Queen.

Her visit meant that Hashem had answered my prayer. The *passuk* says, "Cast your bread upon the waters and in many days it will return to you" (*Koheles* 11:1) and the Midrash says that this is referring to prayer.

Although it was unknown to me at the time, Nellie's visit would bridge the gap between our past and my future. Throughout our childhood Nellie was the religious one, totally committed to prayer and act of kindness. I was more academic and viewed her actions with skepticism. *What is this thing that occupies all her time?* I used to wonder. *What a waste.*

However, now that our roles were wholly reversed, I realized that it was her steadfastness at such a tender early age that had led my soul to search out the *emes*. Maybe we weren't so different after all. There was just an appointed time for the spiritual seeds that she had planted to sprout in my life.

There are various times in the Torah that man is compared to a tree. Praise God, her example has caused my leaves to sprout forth and for me to spring forth in *shirah*.

The fruit that I have brought forth represents a family legacy to me, because Hashem gave me great role models like my mother, my grandmother, and Nellie to pattern my life after. How rich and rewarding my life has become, traveling the world and inspiring Jews to daven and say *Tehillim*.

The day of Nellie's arrival, I was filled with excitement; finally she would get to see with her own eyes the people and country that were so dear to my heart. The day was jam-packed with errands and telephone calls, but I managed to remain calm, anticipating the plane's arrival.

I picked up some flowers and got into a taxi to go to the airport. Upon my arrival, Nellie was nowhere to be found. Nervously peering through the crowds of people, I spotted Dr. Queen. After I greeted him, a familiar sweet voice behind me said, "Hey there!"

It was Nellie. We embraced, almost crushing the flowers. Wouldn't you know it — with all my years of airline experience, I managed to come late to meet her because their plane had arrived early.

The group was leaving for a hotel in Netanyah. After Nellie had gotten settled on the bus, I left her. My parting words to

Shalom Pollack, the veteran tour guide of twenty-eight years, were, "Please take good care of my sister."

After dinner I called her hotel and she was excited because she had already been to Yafo.

"Wasn't it magnificent?" I asked.

"It was fascinating to see the ancient port of Yafo and unbelievable that its history relates to all three major religions."

"You're absolutely right! I studied Yafo's history in my tour guide course, and it spans over four thousand years. Its history goes back almost two thousand years before the Common Era — it's mentioned in ancient records of the pharaohs! In the book of Chronicles it is recorded that when King Solomon purchased the cedars of Lebanon, for the building of the First Temple, those trees were brought by floats to the Yafo port. The first time I read that story in the Bible I tried envisioning the port of Yafo. I never dreamt that one day I would actually see it with my own eyes."

I read my sister's itinerary and continued, "Tomorrow will be even more exciting because you're going to Mount Carmel, where Elijah slew the four hundred false prophets. You'll love the sites from the top of Mount Carmel. There's a panoramic view of the Haifa Bay on one side and the Jezre'el Valley on the other."

I was so excited and grateful that Nellie was in my beloved Eretz Yisrael that I could not stop bubbling. I wanted to share all the facts I knew about the area with her, but I knew she must be tired, so I said, "Get some rest and I'll speak to you after breakfast tomorrow. Good-bye."

"Good night, Delores," she said, addressing me by my English name.

Our Rabbis, of blessed memory, say that the Hebrew letters contain creative power, and when God spoke the Hebrew words the world came into being. So too, I thought, with me. Saying the prayers in Hebrew really brought me to life. That's why Rebbetzin Heyman was always encouraging me to pronounce the Hebrew words properly when reciting the prayers. Hebrew prayers had attracted me and drawn me to Judaism. The very letters of the Hebrew words in my siddur had transformed my life.

Somehow, I felt that my intense davening to share my love for Eretz Yisrael with my sister had infused these moments with special meaning. The culmination of those prayers was my sister, Nellie — here in Israel, at last! Thanks to the Almighty here we were in our adult life sharing a common bond in the land of my spiritual ancestors.

Israel is also the land of my present family and friends, and I was thrilled that at the conclusion of her pilgrimage tour, Nellie still had a few days left to spend with me in my home place. Moreover, Bayit Vegan was eagerly waiting to meet my sister.

When the bell rang that Wednesday evening, my heart began beating rapidly as I ran down the stairs. By mistake Nellie had knocked on my neighbors' door and they were already welcoming her. She walked up the spiral stairs leading to my apartment and entered, glancing curiously at my bookcase standing there. She set her luggage down in the living room and took notice of the other bookcases. Looking puzzled, she asked, "Where are all your secular books?" And indeed, there were only Hebrew books on the shelves.

Since my conversion was completed I had never really explained Jewish law to my family, because they have no frame of reference for such details in their religion, and it just seemed too difficult to start explaining it to them. Nellie knew I had always loved reading and had often seen me take an ordinary book, mark it up with highlighters, and write down thought-provoking questions in the margins.

I tried to explain to Nellie that in order for me to learn and absorb all the teachings in Judaism and to implement them in my life, I felt that I had to study *sifrei kodesh*, holy books, in Hebrew, because the meaning is so often lost in translation. I wasn't sure whether or not she understood how difficult this was for me, and how important, but we dropped the topic and began to enjoy the stir-fried vegetables and rice that I had prepared.

During the meal the conversation shifted from the beautiful sites Nellie had visited in Israel to her concept of "the poor Palestinians." I was tempted to let her comments pass me by, because the last thing that I wanted was a lengthy, heated discussion on the Israeli/Palestinian conflict. We only had a few precious days together — how my soul had longed for this moment!

But I could feel my blood pressure beginning to rise and I simply couldn't let her comments go by. With my voice shaking slightly, I felt compelled to answer: "Nellie, your concerns are typical because Americans are always compassionate for the underprivileged. However, it isn't the Jews' fault that the Palestinians are poor. It's because their government is so corrupt. Do you realize how hard we pray every day for peace and how many innocent children and adults are blown up by their fanatical regime?

"Why don't you try reading a bit more on the situation and

then we could discuss it more intelligently and in depth? In fact, I have several books from my tour guide course that you might find helpful."

"Delores, I had never thought of it that way before. If you feel the books would be beneficial, then I would like to read them."

We quietly dropped the subject, and I telephoned the family in the States to let them know that Nellie had arrived safely to my home. They were excited and full of questions that Nellie tried her best to answer.

All was peaceful when we retired for bed. But before drifting off to sleep I thought, here we were, two sisters, a Christian and Jew, sharing a few days in a Torah-observant neighborhood in Jerusalem. Though political and religious differences might be inevitable, still we could bridge our differences through dialogue and mutual respect. So when I finished davening the bedtime prayer I whispered, "Hashem, please don't let us get into any great theological debates."

The next morning, I began to play "tour guide" in our neighborhood. Perhaps it didn't have as long a history as Yafo, but Bayit Vegan surely had its points of interest, as well.

As we started to walk down the tree-lined streets surging with people shopping for Shabbos, my mind wandered back to when we were children. Nellie would hold my hand as we crossed the street going to the store, and we used to play a children's game called "Follow the Leader." Because she was my senior, it was appropriate to follow her lead. This time Nellie was following my lead to our first stop — the butcher, Rosenbaum. Then we went by the vegetable stand and the grocery store. At the grocer's an amazing thing occurred. There happened to be a particular individual in our neighborhood who never smiled. But when he met Nellie, with her warm, outgoing personality, he actually gave her a great big grin. I guess he just couldn't help being friendly. After we had left the store I explained my astonishment to my sister and remarked, "You should visit more often."

Afterwards we bought flowers and wine for our host families for Shabbos. Everyone greeted Nellie with warm, friendly smiles and courteous hellos as we walked down the street.

The next day, Nellie helped me prepare the house for Shabbos. At candle lighting time, Nellie expressed a wish to light the Shabbos candles, but without a *berachah*. After the lighting, we left for the Schwartzbaums, our hosts for Friday night dinner.

As we walked, Nellie, asked, "What is it that I feel?"

"It's the *kedushah*, holiness, of the Shabbos." How wonderful to know that she was able to sense this.

Our Friday night Shabbos meal with the Schwartzbaums surpassed my greatest expectations. Nellie seemed to thoroughly enjoy the songs that Avraham and the boys sang. She also commented on the delicious dinner and the homemade challos.

When we took leave of the family, we again thanked Rochel for the lovely dinner. Nellie gave her a warm hug and just at that moment I remembered that I had forgotten to tell her not to shake hands with the men. Intervening just in time by stepping in front of her, I explained that women didn't shake hands with men in Orthodox Judaism as they did in her world.

Walking home, Nellie remarked how much she had enjoyed

the men singing. It suddenly occurred to me that this was the first time she had been in a home where men and women didn't sing together. A very different kind of *shirah*, indeed.

On Shabbos morning, I really came to a higher level of appreciation for Nellie's fine character. We woke at 6:30 a.m. to go to HaGra shul for the 7:00 a.m. Shabbos morning service. We hiked up to the women's gallery on the third floor, entered, and took our seats. Rebbetzin Heyman sat on my right and Nellie was on my left. Even though she couldn't speak or understand a word of Hebrew, Nellie sat contentedly for two-and-a-half hours. Every time we stood up during the prayers, I motioned for her to remain seated. I was grateful that she had followed my advice and brought a nice book to read.

At the end of the service, I was sure Nellie was relieved that her ordeal was over. I introduced her to Rebbetzin Heyman and numerous other women in shul, who all accepted her with warm affection. They showed their happiness that my sister was there with me. *Kol hakavod* to HaGra shul! They treated her with respect and made her feel like an honored guest.

As we walked down the stairs my mind wandered back to the first Rosh HaShanah service after my conversion. As we were leaving shul, Rebbetzin Heyman looked at me, having watched me suffer through the intense davening, and said, "Now you understand why we discourage people from converting."

Too drained to answer in any detail, I replied succinctly, "Would you want to deprive me of something so beautiful?"

We spent the rest of the day basking in the physical and spiritual richness of a Bayit Vegan Shabbos. We enjoyed Shabbos lunch with James and Tonia Frohwein, appreciating the good food, *divrei Torah* told over as simply as possible for the sake of my sister, songs, and that special spice of Shabbos that makes even the air taste better and gives "*taam*" to every moment. Nellie loved meeting the special people who had become part of my life. She especially enjoyed the liveliness of Dr. Daniel and Devorah Sheril's children at the third meal. It was a delight to see her joining in and playing games with them. Watching her reminded me of the time when we used to play hopscotch as little girls. My, how we had both hopscotched a long way from home.

After we heard Havdalah, we began walking home. Nellie said, "What a peaceful way to end the Shabbos." Then she asked with a smile, "How do you maintain your weight after eating three such elaborate meals each week?"

"We don't," I replied with a sigh and a laugh.

Once we arrived back at my apartment, it was time to get all of Nellie's personal belongings together for her departure to the States. As we waited for the taxi, Nellie thanked me warmly for the lovely visit. Her words were music to my heart.

When the cab arrived I assisted her with the luggage and we again embraced. She promised to call upon her arrival home. True to her word, she called the next day to let me know she had arrived safely.

A few days later I received this lovely e-mail:

Hi, Ahuvah.

It was truly a pleasurable experience to visit you and witness how you have adjusted to your new home. It was great to finally meet all those families that you are so close to.

I have called everyone in the family since returning and told them that when we see the sensational stories on the nightly news, we don't have to worry about you.

I feel that you have truly found your niche in Bayit Vegan. I have never experienced such love and acceptance as I did from those lovely families in your neighborhood. I am very proud of you that you only have Hebrew books in your home.

After reading Nellie's e-mail I realized that was the first time she had written me using my Hebrew name. Perhaps she simply had to understand the lifestyle of "Ahuvah."

I am sure that my entire transformation hasn't been easy for my family to digest. However, they have done it with much dignity and grace. My brothers called weekly to express their concerns about the *matzav* in Israel. To quote my younger brother, Ezra:

"You be careful over there and pray strongly, and don't forget to pray for us at the Wall, okay, girl?"

I have taken upon myself a new religion, a new name, and a new homeland. Through it all they loved me and supported what was in their opinion my insanity. By being so tolerant they taught me the true meaning of unconditional love. My mother must be so proud of us! Her dream was that her children should value the gift of life and give to others with the utmost dignity. Because of her many good deeds, her words and acts are deeply engraved on our hearts. "Whatever you do in life, do it with dignity." May her legacy continue to flourish as I travel the world and keep her dreams alive.

My sister's visit was a profound lesson in loving tolerance. Nellie was among the few practicing Christians that the *chareidi* families in Bayit Vegan had entertained as a Shabbos guest, and she had been welcomed warmly by everyone.

Who could ever have imagined such a thing? Only the Master of the Universe could orchestrate such a visit. Thank You, Hashem.

It was all for the good that Nellie had come to shul with me because my sister left Israel with a positive outlook on Orthodox Judaism. I pray that *klal Yisrael* will benefit from that lesson and learn to live peacefully with each other, respecting each other's views. It is my prayer that just as He brought a Christian and Jews together peacefully with mutual respect on that Shabbos, He will soon bring all the Jews together in the same vein. At her departure, I envisioned Nellie as an emissary, saying about us, the chosen people, "Is there anything too hard for God?"

But it wasn't only Nellie who gained from her short trip to Bayit Vegan. New vistas seemed to open up to me during my davening the morning after Nellie's departure. We had established a much deeper bond between ourselves and had resolved some of the intricate differences of our views on life. Moreover, my own davening seemed enhanced; my relationship with God, who had granted me the blessing of a family who could remain family even once I left it, was deepened, made closer. I enjoyed knowing that the songs of David HaMelech that Nellie and I had learned together were shared by us; but I could appreciate even more that I could learn the real meaning of those songs from my teachers and could even understand them more fully by reading commentaries in my own Hebrew *sefarim*. In pointing to what we shared and what I had acquired, and in expressing my personal gratitude to God for both those blessings, my sister's visit truly was my personal *shirah*.

Chapter Thirteen

Forty Days at the Kosel

*T*he rocks of the Kosel fascinated me from the first time I saw them and touched the cool surface rubbed smooth by the hands of countless people at prayer. Even though I was a Christian at the time, I felt their power. Although the tour guide explained that it was originally a retaining wall and the least significant in terms of structure, to me it remained the holiest site possible. Here stood the place of the Holy Temple — here stands a wall watered by tears of hearts and souls sharing their needs with God.

My first visit to the Kosel was also my first encounter with such an awesome level of *kedushah*. Even though I wasn't Jewish, when it was time to depart, I kissed the stones, quoted some *Tehillim*, and started to back away. I wanted the memory of this beautiful site with the plants growing out of the stones and the doves lodging on them to stay embedded in my thoughts. I didn't know at that time that it was protocol for religious Jews to back away from the wall. As I left, I knew that this was a place that I would always carry in the deepest chamber of my heart.

I had read many books about the Temple, the holiest site in the world. I knew that it was designed so that it met the spiritual needs of the Jewish people, and that the *Shechinah*, God's holy presence, rested there. At that time these were just words in books; I didn't really know what any of it meant. Now that I am a Jew, I appreciate these concepts in a much more personal way. I also understand now that the Kosel rocks hold within them the hope that the Temple will be rebuilt soon, when Mashiach comes.

And now I comprehend on a much deeper level the significance of the rebuilding of the Beis HaMikdash. On Friday nights we sing *Tzur MiShelo*, a song whose closing stanza says:

May the Temple be rebuilt; the City of Zion replenished.
There we shall sing a new song, with joyous singing ascend.
May the Merciful, the Sanctified, be blessed and exalted
Over a full cup of wine worthy of Hashem's blessing.

This song expresses the essence of what we as the Jewish people look forward to, the return of the *Shechinah*, world peace, and the fullness of Torah knowledge. On a spiritual level it epitomizes all that we long for as Jews. The question that always lingers in my mind is how do we make it happen. I believe it's through our *tefillos* and crying out to Hashem — at the Kosel and in every "*mikdash me'at*," the small sanctuary that every shul and every Jewish home is.

For there is a beautiful parallel between a Jewish home and the Beis HaMikdash. Both are said to be the dwelling place of the Divine Presence. The Temple is the spiritual focal point for the entire nation. The home is the place where the individual practices his unique divine service.

That is why I decided to undertake the task of davening at the Kosel for forty days. I wanted to ask Hashem to help me find my soulmate so that I could make my home into a *mikdash me'at*, a miniature sanctuary, with Hashem's help. Here is how it happened.

A dear friend, Esther Rivkah, visited my home and spoke of the tradition of davening at the Kosel for forty consecutive days. I listened closely, startled, for she had no idea that I had been contemplating that very task. As we sat down to lunch, she shared her own experience with me.

"My former roommate convinced me to daven at the Kosel for forty days. She never out-and-out said anything to me, but I watched her when her first engagement was canceled after the *vort*. She didn't allow herself to be overwhelmed by the situation, but had complete *emunah* and *bitachon* that Hashem would send the right one. Shortly after her forty days of davening, Ahuvah, she got engaged. It was then that I decided to start."

Before she finished, I knew in my heart that I was willing to make the commitment. "It's a special *segulah*, Ahuvah. It changed my entire life and gave me an inner clarity I never before experienced."

Even though she was much younger than I, her words gave me new hope. I had literally traveled around the world and had been on dates in the majority of the countries I visited. When I was leaving Melbourne, after two dates, I remember saying to Hashem: "Is the guy anywhere out there in the universe?" As the airplanes kept ascending and descending, so did my prospects and my hopes.

The next day, I spoke to Rebbetzin Heyman and told her of my plan. This was at the height of the new Intifada, and her main concern was my safety. "You must go by taxi," she said emphatically. "Let me see what I can do." Within forty-eight hours, she called me back. "Ezra Ma'or is going to take you. He's the driver for Rabbi Yitzchak Yerucham Borodiansky, the *mashgiach* of Kol Torah."

I was so excited, I hardly knew what to say. (Ezra later became my regular taxi driver.) "Rebbetzin, I won't forget this. Thank you so much."

"Ahuvahleh, Hashem should answer your prayers. He should send you the right one at the right time, with His *berachos*. I want to marry you off already!"

I started davening at the Kosel on *erev Shabbos*, December 27, 2002. Ezra had arrived promptly at 12:30 p.m. to pick me up. A tenth generation Yerushalmi, he had lovely stories to share, making for an especially pleasant ride.

"Ahuvah, you know the *rebbetzin* says that you are her daughter," he told me on that first day. "She said that I had to give you a very special price, so I did, because who can argue or disagree with the *rebbetzin*?"

As Ezra began to share his background with me, I listened attentively.

"My family owns businesses and houses all over Jerusalem. In the old days, there was no such thing as a Jew afraid of going to East Jerusalem. I grew up with the Arabs and speak Arabic.

"In 1910 and 1911, the Turks began drafting Jews in Palestine to fight against the British. They drafted my paternal grandfather and his uncle, who was a Kabbalist. Before my grandfather left, my grandmother said to him, 'One does not come back alive from there.' She gave him two gold coins, worth about a thousand dollars each, and told him that he should flee to Alexandria, Egypt, where her sister lived. When he got there he should send her a message and she would join him with their son until the war was over and they could return to their beloved Eretz Yisrael.

"My grandfather and his uncle were taken by foot to Atlit (about ten kilometers from Haifa); the Turkish officers kept hitting them with sticks to keep them moving. When they reached Atlit, the Turks forbade all religious practice. They said that anyone who put on tefillin would be shot. My grandfather didn't put on tefillin — he had a wife and son to care for — but the uncle didn't care about death, so he did put on tefillin. He was caught by a Turkish officer, who grabbed the tefillin and threw them on the ground, telling my grandfather's uncle that he would be shot the next day. The uncle looked up to Heaven and cursed the officer with special intentions from Kabbalah, wishing him death. That night the officer got dysentery and died.

"The Turkish commander summoned the uncle and told him he was afraid of him and his powers and that he should leave as quickly as possible. The uncle fled.

"My grandfather went to the commander and said, 'I won't curse you if we make a deal. I'll give you a gold coin and you direct me to Alexandria.' The commander agreed, since he didn't want to take a chance and risk another curse. He told him that there would be a ship leaving the next day, and that he should go to Muhammad, the captain, and give him a gold coin and tell him that the commander sent him.

"My grandfather did just that. Once he reached Alexandria, he went directly to his wife's sister and sent word to his wife that he had arrived safely. She soon joined him in Alexandria along with their son. My grandmother wanted another child, so she prayed in the merit of Rabbi Meir Baal HaNes and vowed that, if she had a son, she would name him Meir and when they returned to Eretz Yisrael she would go every year to the grave of Rabbi Meir Baal HaNes in Teveriah.

"In 1915 she gave birth to a son, my father, and named him Meir. When the war was over, the family returned to Eretz Yisrael, and every year they traveled to the grave of Rabbi Meir Baal HaNes in Teveriah. The trip took three days, by mule, and they would stay a week. They continued that tradition for forty years."

I was so impressed with the story that I was moved to tears. What a family legacy — no wonder he cherished it so much.

Once we arrived at the Kosel, Ezra and I agreed on the time he would return for me and synchronized our watches. Ezra gave me a *berachah* that I should be *matzliach*.

Ezra's punctuality every day reinforced my determination. His stories, too, inspired me to stick with my resolution.

As the days passed, I came to appreciate the Kosel more and more. Oddly enough, my feelings towards my own neighborhood, Bayit Vegan, deepened as well. Perhaps my connection to the Kosel, our holiest place, made me more sensitive to the *kedushah* of my own chosen home.

The first week of my davening at the Kosel, I followed my normal routine of praying three times daily. *Shacharis* at home; *minchah* at the Kosel; and *maariv* as well as the five *Tehillim* for the *matzav* in Israel back home. I was also instructed to recite five *Tehillim* for a *zivug* (soul mate), which I did on the way home from the Kosel.

Over time, I realized that my strength was dwindling and that my twenty-minute *minchah* at the Kosel every day was for me as powerful as a concentrated Rosh HaShanah and Yom Kippur davening. Each day during the return drive to Bayit Vegan I continued to recite the five *Tehillim* for the *matzav* in Israel. Soon, however, the intensity of my feelings had nearly drained me of the strength, and it took everything I had in me to daven *maariv* and recite the bedtime prayer.

On the Jewish calendar the day I started davening was the twenty-third of Shevat. The weekly Torah reading was *Shemos*. Besides davening for my *bashert*, I took on the *segulos* of lighting two candles daily and giving a specific amount to *tzedakah*.

Shevat is the month in which the Jewish people celebrate Tu B'Shvat, the new year of the trees. Even though the ground is hard and cold, and the bark of the tree appears dry, we begin to see a few green leaves sprouting on the trees.

During this time of year, the trees appear lifeless on the outside, while on the inside the sap is beginning to rise. Our Sages compare man to a tree, and so it felt to me: everything appeared wintry on the outside, but my prayer was the sap within me that would rise and nourish my soul.

That week's Torah reading, *Shemos*, described how Pharoah had increased the burden of the Jewish people. I wondered how it fit in with my image of the tree's growth and development and how it related to my resolution. Didn't the picture of a tree beginning to bloom contradict the image of a nation bent over with additional suffering? After some thought, I realized that in some way the same thing that had happened to the Jews in *Shemos* was happening to me. *Shemos* deals with the servitude of *klal Yisrael* and the need for an extra burden before redemption.

I was hopeful that even though I had undertaken more responsibilities, an additional burden, Hashem would give me the strength to succeed in my service to Him.

I had come to realize that all our challenges are a gift from Him and are packaged in such a personalized way to give us strength. As we overcome weaknesses with His help, we become stronger. Now I realized that the image of the tree suggested by Tu B'Shvat and that of the burdens forced upon the Jewish people taken from the parashah weren't in opposition to each other at all. Rather, they were working together. With struggle comes growth.

In my early stages of davening at the Kosel, my struggle for new growth was hidden, just like the sap. Can a tree feel? If it could, it would feel the same sense of growth and transformation that I felt during those forty days as my own sap began to rise. Ironically, with that sense of redemption I could now grasp on a deeper level how the struggle of the Jews in Egypt for a new life related to me. Ultimately, I too, like a tree, like a nation, would have new life and a rebirthing, through burdens and struggle.

My commitment to pray daily at the Kosel proved taxing because of my existing schedule. But just as the tree produces the sap for its own nourishment, my daily travail was nourishing my spiritual vitality. Outwardly, I couldn't see any significant change, but in the inner chamber of my soul the daily prayers at the Kosel were indeed nourishing me — just like the trees.

Then I thought about the *passuk* in *Tehillim* that speaks of the inner chamber as the domain of the Jewish woman. My prayer was that my noble task of davening for forty days at the Kosel would prepare me to be the kind of person described in

Tehillim (45:14): *"Kol kevudah bas melech penimah* — The complete glory of the princess is within." Our Rabbis, of blessed memory, cite this verse as a description for the chastity and modesty of the Jewish woman. She is a princess because she is the daughter of the King. The glory of the Jewish wife and mother is to hold court in the inner chambers of her own home, which is her palace.

Chapter Fourteen

The Weeks of Repentance

$\mathcal{E}$arly in my forty days of davening, I felt no instant growth, nor was I aware of sprouts. However, as I continued to pray at the Kosel, I knew that my soul was being nourished through my hard labor, which reminded me of the hard labor of the Jews in *Shemos*. They were commanded to make bricks without straw, and, God willing, I was laying new spiritual foundations for my life, with the help of the Architect of the world.

The second week's parashah was *Va'eira*, in which Hashem reveals Himself to Moshe as *Keil Shakai*, the Sufficient One. My prayer was that Hashem would give me His sufficient strength to complete my undertaking. When I did my daily exercises that week, I developed a problem that needed medical attention. I made an appointment with Dr. Pinchas Osher, who took care of the problem and ordered me to discontinue my swimming aerobics until the area healed. I was sure that in a week everything would be fine.

Since the rainy season was upon us, walking was impossible, so I really cherished and thus missed the swimming aerobics. I harnessed all my physical, emotional, and intellectual stamina to focus completely on my davening at the Kosel. It became my daily exercise. What is it that the fitness experts say? "Feel the burn" — I felt the warmth of the rocks of the Kosel and the heat that it engendered in my heart and in my soul.

As a result of this experience, aspects of my life were beginning to reveal themselves. I began to understand the following idea that I read in *A Time for All Things*, by Rabbi Nachman Cohen (New York: Torah Lishmah Institute, 1985).

The parashiyos of *Shemos* to *Mishpatim* are known by the acronym *"Shovevim,"* which relates to the word *teshuvah*, repentance. Rabbi Cohen states that during a leap year this period is considered to be one of *teshuvah*. Our Rabbis, of blessed memory, held that in a leap year these weeks contain special properties by virtue of their falling after the winter solstice, the shortest day of the year.

It is said that when Adam sinned, the days were shortened. Adam understood that this occurred because of his sin, and he therefore spent 130 years repenting. What I found very interesting is that usually during the leap year, there are 130 days from the beginning of the *Shovevim* till the end of Pesach.

The book also stated that this period is an *eis ratzon*, a period during which entreaties are accepted. I began to understand why this entire period related specifically to *teshuvah*, especially that of Adam for eating from the Tree of Knowledge.

It was during *Shemos* that I had taken upon myself to daven at the Kosel for forty days. I remembered learning at Neve that during the *teshuvah* process one must be prepared to accept *yissurim*. Then I realized that it is not the outer manifestation of *teshuvah* that is sought; rather, the goal of *teshuvah* is to bring about change in our innermost selves. I have found that the more I daven, the closer I feel to Hashem, and the closer I am to Him the more I understand myself. It's through this process of understanding the essence of my true purpose and meaning in life that I came to do inner *teshuvah*. But I have to be in touch with my true inner feelings as I continue to seek Hashem's will.

As I continued my davening at the Kosel, the inner chamber of my soul was beginning to flourish. I hoped that my inner *teshuvah* was working. By davening and asking Hashem to forgive me of known sins and unknown sins against people I had hurt, either intentionally or unintentionally, I was free to move forward in my life and accept His future blessings.

I was feeling very drained physically and desperately wanted to resume my water aerobics classes. But the first week of healing was not enough; the doctor said I needed to stay away from the pool for another week and then come back to see him again.

By the third week, I thought surely the area would have properly healed. I even took my swimming bag with me to the doctor's office, praying that the doctor would lift his restriction. But after Dr. Osher completed the examination, the answer was no. My heart sank like a rock in the pool that I so longed to be floating in. My disappointment was obvious.

The doctor compassionately shared the following *midrash* with me.

"Come let us demonstrate the difference between a king of flesh and blood and the King of Kings, the Holy One, blessed be He: When a human king wishes to imprison one of his subjects, he requires stones, cement, iron bars, locks and keys, guards, weapons, etc. The Holy One, blessed be He, needs no such paraphernalia. His armory is varied and boundless. He can send a small microbe, which unseen invades the bodily defenses of man. The multiplication of this microbe in a man's person can cause an illness, which essentially neutralizes his daily functions. He may suffer an illness with fever, pain, general malaise, and retires to his sickbed as a prisoner. If it is the Will of Hashem, he may merit through repentance to be healed. While he is ill, Hashem may send him complete healing, with or without a visible agent."

Okay, the doctor's orders against swimming weren't a matter of life and death, but they were enough of a change in my daily routine to make me feel like a prisoner. Whatever microscopic body was slowing down my healing had been sent for a purpose; and the purpose, it seemed to me, was to immerse me in my davening as in a beautiful clear pool and to encourage my inner process of *teshuvah*. In that week's parashah, *Bo*, God Himself carries out the plague against Pharoah. Thank God, my warning was much gentler, and, more thanks to Him, unlike Pharoah with his hard heart, I understood the message of repentance.

At last Dr. Osher declared me to be healed. He had a wide smile on his face and said, "You're fine, Ahuvah. Enjoy your swim." When my dear friend Sheina Medwed picked me up at the bus stop across from the clinic, we laughed all the way to the pool.

"Welcome back, girl," she said. "We missed you. I missed my soul sister in the water!" She was as giddy as I was about my return to swimming.

Though I was a bit stiff and had to work a little harder to

keep up the pace, it was wonderful to be back in the water again.

Tuesday of that week was a routine day, except for the rain. Ezra called me to say that due to the rain, the trip to the Kosel would probably take us twice the time. Despite the downpour, we made good time. When we arrived, Ezra said I need not hurry. I began davening as usual, but that day something was different. As satisfying as the routine had become, davening that day, even in the rain, was especially sweet. I didn't allow myself to be distracted or hampered by the rain. My soul rejoiced on the inside, breaking into song.

Seizing the moment I listened to the melody of the inner chamber of my heart, remembering the verse in Malachi that says: "See if I do not open up for you the windows of the heaven and pour out upon you blessing without end" (*Malachi* 3:10). This was my day to receive.

Finishing a bit beyond the designated time, I walked very quickly toward the entrance where Ezra was waiting. I apologized for being late and added, because I could hardly contain myself, "Ezra, I believe every one of those prayers has been answered."

There was quiet for a moment and then Ezra began to sing, and I started laughing as usual. When he finished singing and I stopped laughing, Ezra said, "I believe it, too, Ahuvah, and I am part of the mitzvah with you." I would realize only weeks later, after I had completed the forty days of davening, how deeply this parashah would touch the inner chamber of my soul.

The Torah reading that week was *Beshalach,* in which Pharoah sent out the children of Israel. Moshe and the children of Israel sing the "Song of the Sea" to Hashem. The second verse of the Song states, "This is my God and I will build Him a sanctuary; the God of my father and I will exalt Him" (*Shemos* 15:2).

I had begun to thoroughly enjoy my davening at the Kosel, especially *erev Shabbos* and *motza'ei Shabbos*. For me, it added a deeper dimension to my Shabbos. Before I began my forty-day commitment, I had asked a *she'eilah* about the six Shabbosos, when I didn't want to be out of my home neighborhood. I was told that I could go by the regular twenty-four hour calendar instead of the Hebrew calendar. I was thus able to make my Kosel visit on Friday, *erev Shabbos*, and then on Shabbos night, *motza'ei Shabbos*, and in that way I could stay home for Shabbos.

Usually on *erev Shabbos* Ezra would park the taxi and we would walk quickly, almost running, to the Kosel entrance. Then Ezra would head to the men's side and I to the women's side. This time Ezra was excited because HaRav Ovadia Yosef, his rebbe, was there. It was my turn to say, "No need to hurry."

When I finished davening, I stood at the entrance next to a woman who gave me a lovely smile. She asked if I was Ahuvah Gray, and when I said yes, she said, "I read your book. You know, when you are davening at the Kosel try going over to the tunnel. It's the part of the Wall closest to the Kodesh HaKodashim."

I thanked her for reminding me about the tunnel, a recently excavated area opposite where the Beis HaMikdash once stood. I hadn't been inside the tunnel since my tour guide course and had totally forgotten about the inner chamber for prayer that was there. But I remembered the special feeling of being in such a holy place the first time.

As I waited for Ezra, I quoted my parents' favorite chapters of *Tehillim*. Psalm 27 was my mother's favorite: "The Lord is my light and my salvation." Psalm 24 was my father's: "The earth is the Lord's and the fullness thereof." Surely on some level I was beginning to understand His fullness as it relates to davening and *Tehillim*.

Ezra arrived about ten minutes later, thrilled because he had spoken with Rav Ovadia Yosef. He apologized for keeping me waiting, but there really was no need for him to apologize because my time had been well spent, too. Ezra always had some meaningful words to share with me; this day, he said, "Ahuvah, you know we have a tradition that every Jewish *neshamah*, past, present, and future, is present at the Kosel."

"I believe you, Ezra. That's why it's so powerful davening here. I felt it the first time I visited there, even before I became a Jew." I told Ezra about my conversation with the lovely lady, whose name I didn't even know, pointing me to the inner chamber.

From that day on, I went into the tunnel to daven.

Chapter Fifteen

The Inner Chamber

The next week's parashah was *Yisro*. It tells us how Moshe Rabbeinu's gentile father-in-law heard about the parting of the Reed Sea, as well as about the Jews' war with Amalek. Recognizing that there was One Supreme Being controlling the entire world, Yisro went out to meet Moshe and then accepted the Torah. The Torah records that Moshe told Yisro all about what had happened to them, and Yisro responded, "*Baruch Hashem.*" He was the first person in history to say those words.

It always fascinated me that a gentile would be the first to say those words. I believe that Yisro underwent what I was about to experience. He must have understood all those events from a place deep within him, his inner ear.

One day well into my forty-day commitment, though I davened as usual, I found I couldn't contain my tears. I had tapped into a deep pain and begged Hashem to remove it. The pain that lingered deep in my heart was anger towards two individuals who had hurt me terribly and deeply many years before.

I had to pray and listen with my inner ear to reach its core. I learned this technique several years ago after the loss of my mother. The only thing that eased the pain was to listen with my inner ear, getting in touch with the core of my feelings, and to sit very quietly and focus in on the feeling, harnessing my thoughts so that I was not distracted by the sounds around me. Then I would carefully scrutinize the words of *Tehillim* and various *pesukim* in *Mishlei* and *Koheles* that comforted my soul.

However, this time the feeling that was tugging away at my *kishkes* was different; this time I had to come to terms with my own anger. During these quiet moments of introspection, a *passuk* in *Mishlei* rose up in my soul: "One who is slow to anger is better than a mighty man, and one who rules over his spirit is better than one who conquers a city" (*Mishlei* 16:32).

Once I was able to identify the feeling, I knew that I needed to get rid of it. The method I used for harnessing this feeling was to identify its source by asking in my mind, "Hashem, who am I angry with?" This is all done silently without uttering a word, and then slowly, slowly the answer comes.

Wisdom comes through knowing the word of God and storing it away in your heart. As the Psalmist states: "In my heart I have stored Your word, so that I would not sin against You" (*Tehillim* 119:11). Then at the appropriate time the *emes* that is needed to resolve the conflict is very close to us, as it is written: "The word is near you, even in your mouth and in your heart," (*Devarim* 31:14). I am so grateful to Hashem for guiding me through this process.

As I sat trying to understand and overcome my anger, I suddenly realized that the men were davening the prayers of Yom Kippur Katan — a very special davening of the day before Rosh

Chodesh, which our Rabbis call a miniature day of atonement. The tradition is to pray *selichos* (prayers for *teshuvah*) after davening *minchah*. The small room in the inner chamber was filled with men and women saying *selichos* with Sephardic accents. I was transported in time to the High Holidays. How wonderful it was for Hashem to remove my anger at such a spiritually high time, to teach me to forgive as I listened to the prayers begging for God's forgiveness. I knew that I was already late in departing, but who could leave the tunnel, so close to the site of the Kodesh HaKodashim, where God would show His forgiveness when the high priest emerged alive at the end of Yom Kippur, at a time like this? I knew Ezra would understand and forgive me, and so he did.

The next week's parashah was *Mishpatim*, when Moshe ascends to the mountain to receive the Torah. May Hashem cause us all to ascend.

My last day of davening at the Kosel was a Tuesday. Ezra was his usual jovial self on the ride there, but I felt quite drained. As we neared the Kosel, Ezra saw a car decorated for a wedding, and he said, "Look, a *chasan*." He pulled up next to the car and said, "Please give her a *berachah*. It's her last day of davening forty days at the Kosel."

"Yes, I give her a *berachah* that she should have a good and successful *shidduch*, and a happy life," the *chasan* said kindly.

The last day was particularly special because there was no one else in the tunnel when I went. I had a private audience with the Holy One, blessed be He. I remembered that Rebbetzin Chaya Beer said, "Ahuvah, you have to beg Hashem." I prayed for *parnasah* and *zivugim* for everyone else first and mentioned myself last. The words of the song that Moshe and the children of Israel had sung came to my mind: "This is my God and I will build Him a sanctuary, the God of my father and I will exalt Him" (*Shemos* 15:2). As I walked back to the car I knew in my heart that just as Hashem had sent the Jews out of Egypt as free men and women, He would unshackle me from the chains that had me bound.

When I returned to the car, I said to Ezra, "Thank God we have finished. I am saying 'we' because without help from you, my loyal friend, I simply could not have done this."

Ezra laughed and said, "Yes, yes, Ahuvah, we finished!"

As we began to drive home, Ezra grew serious and began talking about the experience of the last forty days, telling me things that shocked and moved me. "Ahuvah, do you remember the day when we took the two seminary students with us? You had to go back twice to tell them that we had to leave because there was no parking spot. Well, when you went back the second time an Arab came over to me and showed me a coin. He asked if I would like to buy it. When I said no, he pulled a knife on me and I yelled for the police. He ran away.

"And then there was another day when you were giving a tour. You had canceled me because you felt that when you finished the tour you would be somewhere near the Kosel so you would go on your own, but then you called me because you finished early and it was raining hard. I was with Rabbi Yitzchak Yerucham Borodiansky, the *mashgiach* of Kol Torah. When I told the rabbi it was you and that you wanted me to take you to the Kosel, the rabbi said, 'Go take Ahuvah to daven. I will take a taxi home.'

"Wait a minute, Ahuvah, there is more," Ezra continued.

"Remember the other week when you said you felt your prayers were answered? I had been sick that week — I stayed in bed for two days. I couldn't even drive the rabbi that week. When I got out the bed each day to take you to daven, my wife said, 'Where are you going? You are sick!' I told her I had to go because I was part of your mitzvah."

What could I say? There was no way to thank him or compensate him for his selflessness.

I don't know when Hashem is going to answer my prayers and send me my soulmate. Everything happens at the right time, but the privilege of davening for forty days at the Kosel has cleared the inner chamber of my heart and brought me closer to Him. I haven't had a more fulfilling experience in my life. It was a pleasure!

It was Thursday and I had had a jam-packed day. I called Ezra, and as he drove me around to do my errands, he said, "Ahuvah, it's been one year since you did the davening. Do you remember? Exactly one year."

"Yes, I remember, Ezra. How could I forget?"

When Ezra dropped me off at home and I carried all the packages up the stairs, I sat down and said to myself, "Boy, do I remember."

Moments later, my groceries packed away, I went to start looking over the week's parashah. I checked the calendar and saw that this week's parashah was *Yisro.*

I sat quietly and started to read the weekly Torah reading. I knew that there was much discussion about the question of whether Yisro joined the Jews before or after they received the Torah, but that wasn't what I focused on today. Today, one year after I had the wondrous experience of davening forty days at the Kosel, I could think of only one thing: that it was a convert who, upon seeing God's *hashgachah* and His caring for the Jews, first uttered the beautiful words *baruch Hashem*. And I, another convert who experienced *hashgachah* and caring in my life, and especially during those precious forty days, could only echo those words: *Baruch Hashem*.

Postscript

Jewish Geography

ewish geography. You've probably played the game — two Jews meet on a bus or train, in shul, at a store, at a Shabbos dinner and start figuring out who they have in common. You're from Toronto? You must know my cousin...my uncle...my best friend's sister-in-law's brother....

It's a fun game, but it's really a whole lot more than that. Jewish geography is a way of establishing connections, of creating bonds, of underlining the wondrous fact that we Jews are all related. Our history may have spread us to the four corners of the geographic world, but we remain one family — or cousins of cousins of brothers-in-law, at the very least.

When I first joined the Jewish people, Jewish geography was not a game I excelled at. After all, though my *neshamah* was linked to the Jewish people at Har Sinai, though I consider Avraham Avinu, the first *ger*, as my forefather, the reality was that I knew few living Jews and was related by blood or marriage to none. So how could I play?

Over the years, however, I've established my own kind of

Jewish geography. First of all, I have seen the Jewish world in so many parts of the globe. To see a shul on the Rock of Gibraltar, to speak in a day school in Hong Kong, to address Jewish children in London, is to gain new insights into Jewish geography in the most literal sense of those words.

But through the years, I have become expert in the more traditional game of Jewish geography, as well. For I have become close to so many people who have then linked me with others who linked me with others.... I have become familiar with *rabbanim*, with those steeped in wisdom; I have enjoyed friendships at seminaries with girls from the four corners of the world; I have met neighbors in Bayit Vegan who have taken me in like a daughter. Through these relationships I have forged new relationships, met best friends, cousins, sons- and daughters-in-law who have allowed me to share their lives. I have sent best regards from people in one hemisphere to their relatives in another, becoming a link bringing far-flung friends and family members together.

And in my travels, my Jewish geography game expanded and grew. As I traveled the globe, I encountered wonderful Jews who opened their homes and their hearts to me. Somehow, with God's help, my words seemed to inspire them; and with God's help, the welcome I received from these people inspired in me a sense of belonging to a warm and loving family. The family of Jewish geography.

Innumerable people connected to me helped make my travels rich and productive. To write about each one in detail would be to write another book (maybe with God's help, someday...). At the conclusion of this book, which details some of my travels, I would like to mention some of the other places that I spoke at and some of the people who made my visits possible. Some of these people helped organize the trips and the talks. Some welcomed me to their homes or made me a festive meal. Some introduced me before a speech; some calmed me down when I felt nervous speaking before hundreds of strangers; others gave me a reassuring hug when I finished a speech.

What all these people have in common is that they helped enrich my life, made my travels possible, made me feel like part of the expanded Jewish family — and made my place and space part of the world of Jewish geography. To all, my thanks.

- ## West Rogers Park, Chicago, IL
  Thanks to Rabbi Zev Kahn and the entire faculty of the Torah Learning Center.

- ## Skokie, IL
  In Skokie, I lectured for Rabbi Harvey Well at his shul, Or Torah. Many special thanks to my host family Roz and George Bornstein, parents of Matt Bornstein, and to Lynne Shapiro for arranging the lecture.

- ## Boca Raton, FL
  My dear friend Stacey Katz from Neve, who lived in Boca Raton for about two years, kept saying, "Ahuvah, you have got to lecture in Boca Raton." After she moved to Passaic, New Jersey, she was instrumental in setting up my visit one year later.

  My contact was Rabbi Efrem Goldberg, who worked with Rabbi Kenneth Brander, the rabbi of the Boca Raton Synagogue. I stayed with the family of Leah Rosen, a good friend from the Nishmat days.

- ## Baltimore, MD

    So many names I have to mention here! My host family, Rabbi and Rebbetzin Feldman; Miriam Millhauser and her mother, Mrs. Gittle Millhauser, *a"h*; Devorah Goldstein; Danielle Sarah Storch; Naomi Freeman Goldberg; the whole Neve crowd; and the entire team of organizers of the lecture, especially the rabbi of Congregation Shearith Israel, Rabbi Yaakov Hopfer.

- ## Lakewood, NJ

    I must say, there was something thrilling about lecturing in the town that houses one of the greatest centers of Torah learning in America. Thanks to Farrah and Michelle and the whole Hammer family for such wonderful hospitality and to the team of organizers of the fund-raiser for Frances Opatut Junior High School.

- ## Passaic, NJ

    It is so wonderful to have family all over the world. The hospitality of the Korenblit family made me feel part of the family. I loved the relaxed atmosphere and the wonderful Korenblit kids, and it was great seeing all my seminary buddies, Stacey Katz, Judy Cooper, and Diane Pechman. I'm grateful to Hashem for all the lovely young friends He has placed in my life who keep me feeling young even when I am on the road.

- ## Toronto, Ontario

    What a privilege it was to lecture in the Bayit, the largest shul in North America! Arrangements were handled by Ateret book store and Annie Samuels, and I had just a little time to visit with Dr. Joyce and Abraham Morel.

- **Brooklyn, NY**

  I know New Yorkers are supposed to be unfriendly — but never trust stereotypes! I have made warm friendships with so many people who helped me when I spoke in New York. Special thanks go to Judy and Elan Reiser and Rabbi Danny Goldstein of Kingsway Shul and his wife, Jenni.

- **Manhattan, NY**

  Many special thanks to Adam Jacobs, managing director of Aish HaTorah New York, for allowing me many opportunities to grow during the numerous occasions that I have lectured for Aish Upper West Side.

- **Los Angeles, CA**

  A very special thanks to the Fairfax community and Rabbi Avraham Czapnik at Jewish Learning Exchange. My warmest regards to my little sister Elisa Weiss for her hospitality.

- **Dallas, TX**

  Many thanks to Rabbi Yerachmiel Fried and the entire staff at DATA (Dallas Area Torah Association), for the opportunity to lecture at their annual women's conference.

- **San Antonio, TX**

  It was great to visit the city of the Riverwalk, the Alamo, and the Torah Learning Center, the heart of the Jewish community in San Antonio. I lectured for Linda Fisher, director of the San Antonio Association of Jewish Education (SAAJE); Rabbi Aryeh Scheinberg, the rabbi of Congregation Rodfei Sholom; and Rabbi Yossi Sprung, one of the rabbis in the Torah Learning Center (TLC), the *kollel* of San Antonio. Many thanks to my host family, Liz and Mike Lifschitz.

- Antwerp, Belgium

The Fried family took wonderful care of me in this gracious European city. I must mention one woman whose name I don't know but whose remarks I will never forget. After my talk, she came over to me and said, "Rebbetzin Gray, thank you for such an inspirational evening and for giving us new insight into prayer."

I was uncomfortable with her calling me a *rebbetzin*, so I said softly, "I am very happy that you enjoyed the lecture, but I am not a *rebbetzin*."

She protested immediately, "Yes, you are, Ahuvah, because you are teaching Jewish women all over the world the benefit of the Hebrew prayer."

In Belgium, English is the women's second language — but the language of the heart that they spoke was oh, so easy for me to understand.

- London, England

Thirteen lectures in five days — it should have gotten me into the Guinness Book of World Records, or at least gained me a knighthood from Queen Elizabeth. So many people made this possible. Many thanks to Leslie and Albert Bendahan, my host family.

Thanks to Rabbi Shaul Robinson and the entire staff of Encounter, the largest *kiruv* organization in England, for allowing me the privilege of being the keynote speaker before Rabbi Yisrael Meir, Rabbi Jonathan Sachs, Rabbi Akiva

Tatz, and Rabbi Lawrence Kelemen.

• Gibraltar

The Jewish community of Gibraltar is rock solid. Elisheva and Solly Garson and the Copperman family made my stay on the unusual island memorable. They even kept me calm when "the monkeys of the rock," a pack of monkeys searching for food, jumped on our car as I took in the sights, perhaps the most startling incident of all my travels.

• Australia

It would be impossible for me to thank everyone involved in making my lecture tour to Australia a success. However, in addition to the people mentioned above, I must thank Les Brown for assisting me with the book sales following each lecture. I would like to thank the Adass lady who attended a second lecture and shared with me at the end of the lecture that she was reading *Tehillim* with her children because of my grandmother. *Kol hakavod* to my grandmother.

With a humble and grateful heart, I would like to thank everyone who worked on the committee that arranged my lecture tour.

A final word:

So many people helped me along the way, it is almost impossible for me not to have missed some. To those whose names I didn't mention, my apologies. You are in my heart and my mind, and your acts of kindness should be a merit to you always.

Ahuvah

Acknowledgments

I would like to express gratitude and appreciation to the following people:

Rabbi Leib Heyman and Rabbi Aharon Feldman for their halachic advice and countless hours of reading, and Rabbi Emanuel Feldman for his advice on specific chapters.

Rabbi Yosef Ben Shlomo Hakohen, author of *The Universal Jew* and Torah teacher of Hazon: Our Universal Vision, for knowledge on *midrashim*.

Rebbetzin Chaya Heyman for her expertise in grammar and editing as well as motherly advice. A special thanks to Rebbetzin Tziporah Heller for reading the entire manuscript.

Many special thanks to Sheina Medwed, for her prolific creative writing skills and her assistance in adding the finishing touches to the manuscript, and to Sarah Shapiro, for reading the material and encouraging me to become a writer.

Special thanks to all the seminary students from around the world whose vitality gives me *chizuk*, especially Ahuva Taranda, my study partner and close friend, and Sally Abraham and

Shani Borgenicht from London, who inspired me with our weekly *Tehillim* study sessions.

A very special thanks to Rebbetzin Tova Weingot for the privilege of teaching a *Tehillim* class at Shaarei Bina; and appreciation to my dear friend Rena Cohen for her exquisite bed-and-breakfast accommodations in Tzefas, my rest haven away from home. Rabbi Natan and Sheina Gamedze are also deserving of thanks.

I'd like to express my warmest appreciation to my neighborhood, Bayit Vegan, and all the wonderful families that have allowed me to be a part of their families, especially James and Tonia Frohwein, Rabbi and Rebbetzin Aryeh Carmell, Melech and Elaine Lehman, Mr. and Mrs. David Sassoon, and Rabbi Avraham and Avigail Ravitz. A special thanks to Rabbi Tuvia and Chaya Heller for the wonderful Shabbos meals and Tuvia's expertise in designing my website. Many special thanks to all the neighbors in my building for being the best neighbors I've been privileged to enjoy. Special gratitude to my little sister, the Jew, Channa Shapiro, who reads and translates all my Hebrew letters.

I'd like to thank Devorah Rubin, our Chumash teacher, for feeding my *neshamah* and all my classmates for their encouragement: Rochel Schwartzbaum, Leslie Kolbrener, Aviva Freifield, Rochel Solomon, and Chaya Heller.

A special thanks to Dovid Sheril for his research efforts on the *midrashim*. A special thanks to David Landesman, Natan Iskowitz, and Joshua Bennett for their lovely *niggumim* during *Shabbosim* at the Landesman.

I'd like to thank Malka Zwick for her beautiful poems and the wonderful Shabbos meals I was privileged to enjoy in her home in Telz Stone.

To my dear friend Miriam Millhauser for her book entitled *Inner Torah* that inspired me during the completion of this manuscript.

Kol hakavod to my family, Oscar, Ezra Sr. and Ezra Jr., and Nellie for their encouragement and for teaching me loving tolerance.

A very special thanks to all the staff at Targum, especially Mimi Zakon and Rabbi and Mrs. Moshe Dombey. A special thanks to Emmy Zitter for her expertise in the final editing.

Above all, I would like to express my gratitude to Hashem for giving me the strength and ability to share that gift with my readership!

I'd like to thank Rebbetzin Leah Feldman for being a model *eishes chayil* and Rebbetzin Chaya Beer and Rose Kempner for their *tefillos*.

The following words, which we sing on Rosh HaShanah, fully convey my thoughts and feelings for *klal Yisrael* for the loving kindness you have shown me:

> *Chamol al maasecha* — Have compassion on Your handiwork and be glad with Your handiwork. May those who take refuge in You say, when You vindicate those borne by You, "O Master, may You be sanctified upon all Your handiwork." For with Your own holiness You have sanctified those who sanctify You. It is fitting that the Holy One be glorified by holy ones.

The true essence and beauty of this song in its entirety can only be appreciated in Hebrew. I have found that these Hebrew *niggunim* touch the *neshamah* as the Jewish people worldwide have touched my heart and soul.

Glossary

abba — father

a"h — acronym for *aleha hashalom,* may she rest in peace

Amidah — the silent prayer recited three times a day (also referred to as *"Shemoneh Esrei"*) on the weekdays

avodah — service

baruch Hashem — thank God

bashert — intended

beis midrash — study hall

Beis HaMikdash — the Holy Temple

berachah (pl. *berachos*) — blessing

Bereishis — Genesis

bitachon — trust [in God]

challah (pl. challos) — braided bread traditionally eaten on Sabbath and the holidays

Chanukah — Hanukkah

chareidi — ultra-Orthodox

chasan — groom

chas veshalom — Heaven forbid

chein — grace

chizuk — strength

chol — secular, mundane

cholent — a hot dish usually made of meat, potatoes, beans, and barley served on the Sabbath

daven — pray

Devarim — Deuteronomy

d'var Torah (pl. *divrei Torah*) — Torah discourse

eiruv — an enclosure which permits carrying objects outdoors on Sabbath

emes — truth

emunah — faith

Eretz Yisrael — the land of Israel

erev — the day before

eved Hashem — servant of God

frum — religious

gadol — great person (used to refer to a leader and Torah scholar)

gebenched — blessed

ger — convert

hachnasas orchim — hospitality

hakaras hatov — gratitude

halachah (pl. halachos) — law

Har Sinai — Mount Sinai

Hashem — God

hashgachah — supervision

hashgachah peratis — Divine providence

kallah — bride

kavanah — concentration

kedushah — holiness

kesher — connection

Kiddush — the blessing recited over wine on the Sabbath to sanctify the day

kiddush haShem — sanctification of God's Name

kinderlach — children

kishkes — intestines

klal Yisrael — the nation of Israel

kodesh — holy

Kodesh HaKodashim — the Holy of Holies, i.e., the inner chamber of the Temple

kohein (pl. *kohanim*) — priest

kol hakavod — all the honor

kollel — an institution where married men study Torah and receive a stipend

korbanos — sacrifices

Kosel — the Western Wall

l'chaim — a toast (literally, "to life")

lehavdil — to differentiate

luchos — tablets

maariv — evening prayers

makolet — corner grocery store

Mashiach — the Messiah

matzav — situation

matzliach — successful

mazal tov — congratulations

Megillas Eichah — Lamentations

melaveh malkah — a meal on Saturday night which "escorts" the Sabbath out

middos — character traits

midrash — a story taught by the Sages or an explanation of the underlying significance of the Bible text

minchah — afternoon prayers

minhag — custom

Mishlei — Proverbs

Moshe — Moses

navi — Prophets (literally, "prophet")

nechamah — comfort

neshamah (pl. *neshamos*) — soul

niggun (pl. *niggunim*) — tune

parnasah — livelihood

passuk (pl. *pesukim*) — verse

Pirkei Avos — Ethics of the Fathers

rabbanim — rabbis

Rashi — a twelfth century Sage and Torah scholar

rav — rabbi

rebbetzin — a woman of spiritual stature, usually a rabbi's wife

sefer (pl. *sefarim*) — books, especially holy ones

segulah (pl. *segulos*) — spiritual remedy or charm

seudah — festive meal

Shabbaton (pl. *Shabbatonim*) — a Sabbath get-together

Shabbos — Sabbath

Shabbos goy — a gentile who does work for Jews on Sabbath

shacharis — morning prayers

shamash — the candle used to light the other lights of a menorah

Shechinah — the Divine Presence

she'eilah — question

Shema — the fundamental statement of Jewish belief, recited twice a day

Shemoneh Esrei — the silent prayer recited three times a day

Shemos — Exodus

shidduch — match

shirah — song

shul — synagogue

siddur — prayer book

Sukkos — the festival of Tabernacles

taam — taste, flavor

tafkid — purpose, task

talmid (pl. *talmidim*) — student

tefillah (pl. *tefillos*) — prayer

Tehillim — Psalms

teshuvah — repentance

Teveriah — Tiberias

tikun — rectification

Tishah B'Av — the ninth of Av, a day of mourning in commemoration of the loss of the Holy Temple

tzedakah — charity

tzelem Elokim — image of God

Vayikra — Leviticus

vort — engagement party

Yerushalayim — Jerusalem

Yeshayah — Isaiah

yetzer hara — evil inclination

Yiddishe nachas — Jewish pride

Yiddishkeit — Judaism

Yirmiyahu — Jeremiah

zechus — merit

zemiros — songs

zivug (pl. *zivugim*) — soulmate

zt"l — an acronym for *zecher tzaddik levrachah*, may the righteous person's memory be blessed